Activities for Mediation

Building bridges in the ELT classroom

Riccardo Chiappini and Ethan Mansur

| Download the free DELTA Augmented app onto your device | Start picture recognition and scan the **pages with this icon**. | Download files and use them now or save them for later |

Images:
2.1a DELTA Augmented download Shutterstock (Gregory Dean), New York; **U4** Ethan Mansur, Madrid; **U4** Riccardo Chiappini, Madrid; **2.1a DELTA Augmented download** Shutterstock (Prostock-studio), New York; **5** Shutterstock (mashmash_design), New York; **16** Shutterstock (Richcat), New York; **17** Shutterstock (Blan-k), New York; **17** Shutterstock (VectorButtons), New York; **17** Shutterstock (Botond1977), New York; **18** Shutterstock (YoGinta), New York; **18** Shutterstock (pspn), New York; **19** Shutterstock (aiconsmith), New York; **19** Shutterstock (iconim), New York; **20** Shutterstock (U-Design), New York; **20** Shutterstock (Botond1977), New York; **20** Shutterstock (MIKHAIL GRACHIKOV), New York; **21** Shutterstock (bsd), New York; **21** Shutterstock (ober-art), New York; **27** Shutterstock (Aha-Soft), New York; **28** Shutterstock (Tetiana Yurchenko), New York; **29** Shutterstock (Gazlast), New York; **33** Shutterstock (Inked Pixels), New York; **34** Shutterstock (solomon7), New York; **37** Shutterstock (SCOTTCHAN), New York; **37** Shutterstock (Vladvm), New York; **37** Shutterstock (M-SUR), New York; **40** Shutterstock (Tetiana Saienko), New York; **40** Shutterstock (Inspiring), New York; **43** Shutterstock (Inked Pixels), New York; **54** Shutterstock (ANNA ZASIMOVA), New York; **58** Shutterstock (Hand Robot), New York; **58** Shutterstock (New Africa), New York; **58** Shutterstock (unknown1861), New York; **58** Shutterstock (Ruslan Semichev), New York; **63** United States Government; **65** Shutterstock (Dacian G), New York; **66** Shutterstock (meimei studio), New York; **68** Shutterstock (Suthar Naveen P), New York; **74** Shutterstock (paprika), New York; **77** Shutterstock (alexasokol83), New York; **77** Shutterstock (Eugenia Petrovskaya), New York; **81** Shutterstock (Prostock-studio), New York; **82** Shutterstock (George Rudy), New York; **83** Shutterstock (ChetnaC), New York; **94** Shutterstock (Lightspring), New York; **94** Shutterstock (d-e-n-i-s), New York; **95** Shutterstock (howcolour), New York; **98** Shutterstock (Libellule), New York; **105** Shutterstock (PiXXart), New York; **115** Shutterstock (T-Kot), New York; **115** Shutterstock (Osman Vector), New York; **119** Shutterstock (bsd), New York; **122** Shutterstock (tynyuk), New York; **133** Shutterstock (Social Media Hub), New York; **142** Shutterstock (pingebat), New York; **153** Shutterstock (grmarc), New York; **155** Shutterstock (Blan-k), New York; **173** Shutterstock (Bikomins), New York; **177** Shutterstock (Blan-k), New York; **179** Shutterstock (bsd), New York; **179** Shutterstock (Fourdoty), New York; **182** Shutterstock (Black Creator 24), New York

1st edition 1 5 4 3 2 1 | 2025 24 23 22 21
The last figure shown denotes the year of impression.

All rights reserved. No part of this publication may be reproduced, stored in a retrieval system, or transmitted, in any form or by any means, electronic, mechanical, photocopying, recording, or otherwise, without prior written permission from the publisher.

Delta Publishing, 2021
www.deltapublishing.co.uk

© Ernst Klett Sprachen GmbH, Rotebühlstraße 77, 70178 Stuttgart, 2021
www.klett-sprachen.de/delta

Authors: Riccardo Chiappini, Ethan Mansur
Series Editor: Jason Anderson
Editor: Kate Baade
Cover: Andreas Drabarek
Design: Joachim Schrimm, ETYPO, D-71292 Friolzheim
Printing and binding: Plump Druck & Medien GmbH, Rheinbreitbach

ISBN 978-3-12-501744-3

Preface

The DELTA Publishing Ideas in Action series aims to help teachers to relate specific areas of theory and research to their classroom practice. It aims to bridge the divide between these through explanation of the theory from a practitioner perspective, discussion of major research findings and linking both of these to example activities, strategies and suggestions for the classroom. Written by practising teachers and experienced materials writers, Ideas in Action titles show that theory and practice can come together to make English language learning both effective and enjoyable for all.

Mediation has recently become a new "buzzword" in language teaching circles, particularly in Europe, due to the recent development of "can do" descriptors for mediation activities in the Council of Europe's recently updated CEFR (2020). This has established mediation as a key concept in language use, and therefore, also in language learning. This resource book is one of the first to respond to this innovation, offering numerous activities to enable learners to practise mediation skills across all three subcategories of mediating texts, mediating concepts and mediating communication. Not only that, the authors also provide a range of supplementary resources to enable teachers who are new to this way of looking at language use to understand what it is, why it's important and—of greatest value to us as teachers—how to develop learners' proficiency in mediation skills.

While many of us will notice overlaps between the different task and activity types provided in this book and other ways of categorising language use, the fascinating thing about the recent focus on mediation is that it recognises the close relationship between *language use* and *language form*, by which I mean not only form at morphological and syntactical levels, but also aspects of discourse structure, genre and, perhaps most importantly, differences in form between languages – areas largely neglected in teaching materials to date. The recent multilingual turn in education (May, 2013) has brought to the fore the need to focus on both *intralinguistic* and *cross-linguistic* practices (see the authors' Introduction for clarification of these terms); the related concept of "translanguaging" raises our awareness not only of how different languages can be used together flexibly in appropriate contexts (see Anderson, 2018), but also of how even those who were traditionally thought of as "monolinguals" are in fact also capable of translanguaging – in how they use genre types, social norms and even dialects and registers appropriately, all of which involves aspects of mediation.

I am very much impressed by the authors' ability not only to clarify some of the trickier concepts within the mediation literature, but also to provide numerous examples of mediation tasks and activities to ensure that teachers and learners get to grips with it. Not only do the activities included provide the usual photocopiable materials, clear procedure and suggestions for variation typical of the Ideas in Action series, but they also offer concrete suggestions for providing feedback to learners on their performance in tasks, ideas for differentiation, and even suggestions for virtual classrooms – particularly relevant in the "post-Covid" era. Some of my personal favourites are unit **2.1b Debunked**, which offers vital critical literacy skills for the current social media era, and the cross-linguistic skills practised in units such as **2.4d What's on the menu?**. Those of us who work cross-culturally regularly experience the need to understand a menu in a foreign language, yet such skills are rarely, if ever, practised in current global textbooks, which remain predominantly intralingual in their activity orientation.

I sincerely hope you enjoy using **Activities for Mediation**, the fifth addition to the Ideas in Action series, as much as I am sure I will.

Jason Anderson
Series Editor: Ideas in Action

Activities for Mediation – Contents

		Levels of example activities		Page
0	**Introduction to Mediation**			7
1	**Mediation strategies**			16
2	**Mediating a text**			24
2.1	**Mediating a text: Relaying specific information**			24
2.1a	B is for bureaucracy	B1–B2	Translating, paraphrasing, explaining, breaking down complicated information	24
2.1b	Debunked	B2–C1	Selecting and omitting information, paraphrasing, summarising, adapting language	30
2.1c	Flat hunting	A2–B1	Selecting and omitting information, translating, explaining sociocultural elements	35
2.1d	Giving and following instructions	B1–B2	Selecting and omitting information, breaking down complicated information, expanding and/or summarising, paraphrasing	38
2.1e	Multilingual media	B2–C1	Selecting and omitting information, paraphrasing, translating, explaining	41
2.1f	Nail your essay!	B2–C1	Selecting and omitting information, summarising, explaining, paraphrasing	44
2.1g	Travel advice	B1–B2	Selecting and omitting information, translating, explaining sociocultural elements	50
2.2	**Mediating a text: Data and notes**			52
2.2a	Gaming galore	C1–C2	Selecting and omitting information in visual texts, transforming visual information into verbal text, explaining, combining	52
2.2b	Write for me, please	A2–B1	Selecting and omitting information, explaining, summarising	56
2.2c	Elections	B2–C1	Selecting and omitting information, transforming visual data into verbal text, expanding and/or summarising	60
2.2d	Metanotes	B2–C1	Breaking down complicated information, paraphrasing, summarising	65

Activities for Mediation – Contents

		Levels of example activities		Page
2.3	**Mediating a text: Processing texts**			71
2.3a	A fairy tale for children	B2–C1	Selecting and omitting information, adapting language, linking to previous knowledge, paraphrasing, combining	71
2.3b	Cultural (con)version	B1–B2	Selecting and omitting information, paraphrasing, summarising, combining, explaining sociocultural elements	75
2.3c	Tips for new parents	B2–C1	Summarising, paraphrasing, selecting and omitting information	78
2.3d	Running dictogloss	B2–C1	Selecting and omitting information, summarising, paraphrasing, translating	84
2.3e	What should I study?	C1–C2	Selecting and omitting information, summarising, paraphrasing	86
2.4	**Mediating a text: Translating texts**			91
2.4a	Celebrations around the world: Christmas and beyond	B1–B2	Selecting and omitting information, translating, explaining sociocultural and sociolinguistic elements, combining, expanding and/or summarising, paraphrasing	91
2.4b	Online translation doesn't always work	B2–C1	Selecting and omitting information, explaining, linking to previous knowledge, paraphrasing	96
2.4c	Lost property	A2–B1	Selecting and omitting information, translating, explaining, summarising, paraphrasing	99
2.4d	What's on the menu	A2–B1	Translating, linking to previous knowledge, explaining	101
2.4e	Signs and notices	A1–A2	Translating, paraphrasing, explaining	103
2.4f	*SOS* SMS	A2–B1	Selecting and omitting information, translating, explaining, summarising, paraphrasing	105
2.4g	Troubleshooting	B1–B2	Selecting and omitting information, paraphrasing, summarising, adapting language	108
2.5	**Mediating a text: Mediating creative texts**			113
2.5a	Breaking news	B2–C1	Selecting and omitting information, summarising	113
2.5b	Compare and review	B2–C1	Selecting and omitting information, summarising, combining	116

Activities for Mediation – Contents

		Levels of example activities		Page
2.5c	Film feelings	B1–B2	Selecting and omitting information, summarising	120
2.5d	Motives	B2–C1	Selecting and omitting information, summarising	123
2.5e	Tweet me	B2–C1	Summarising	127
3	**Mediating concepts**			130
3a	Black holes	A2–B1	Identifying key information, breaking down complicated information, expanding, summarising, paraphrasing, combining	130
3b	Critical incidents	B2–C1	Summarising, giving examples, linking to previous knowledge, using cultural knowledge	135
3c	First day at work	A2–B1	Explaining, summarising	140
3d	Construction foreman	A2–B1	Explaining, transforming visual data into verbal text, paraphrasing, summarising, combining	144
3e	DIY word formation	B2–C1	Breaking down complicated information, explaining, adapting language	147
3f	Put on your thinking cap(s)	B2–C1	Selecting and omitting information, summarising, explaining	150
4	**Mediating communication**			154
4a	(Inter)mediators	A2–B1	Paraphrasing, summarising, translating, explaining sociocultural elements	154
4b	Conflicts and disagreements	B1–B2	Explaining sociocultural elements, summarising, translating	158
4c	Culture collision	B1–B2	Explaining sociocultural elements, linking to previous knowledge, explaining	161
4d	Debate with moderator	B2–C1	Selecting and omitting information, summarising	163
4e	With a little help "for" my friends	A1–A2	Translating, adapting language, explaining sociocultural elements, paraphrasing, summarising	166
4f	Host family meeting	A2–B1	Explaining sociocultural elements, summarising, combining	169
5	**How to create tasks and adapt materials**			174
6	**Assessing mediation**			179
	References			183

0 Introduction

Introduction to mediation

When you hear the word "mediation," what probably comes to mind is the resolution of commercial, international and personal disputes. However, this term has recently become a buzzword in the world of ELT with the release of the *Companion Volume* to the *Common European Framework of Reference for Languages: Learning, Teaching and Assessment* (CEFRCV). In this document, mediation is defined in the following way:

> "In mediation, the user/learner acts as a social agent who creates bridges and helps to construct or convey meaning, sometimes within the same language, sometimes across modalities (e.g. from spoken to signed or vice versa, in cross-modal communication) and sometimes from one language to another (cross-linguistic mediation)."
>
> Council of Europe (2020, p.90)

Despite the recent interest in mediation, it still doesn't appear by name in most coursebooks and many teachers may be unfamiliar with the concept. The aim of this book is to fill that gap by familiarising teachers with mediation and providing them with a wide variety of mediation tasks for them to use in their classrooms, whether they are teaching in secondary schools, universities or private language schools. We will also provide practical tips on how to teach and assess mediation.

1 A brief history of mediation

Mediation was introduced into mainstream language teaching and learning when it was included in the first version of the CEFR (Council of Europe, 2001). Before this, the term "mediation" was already in use in the field of education, most notably in the works of L. S. Vygotsky, 1978, and later on by the proponents of sociocultural theories of learning (Lantolf, 2000). In the CEFR 2001, however, mediation was given a new, more specific definition in the context of language teaching and learning, which consisted of the everyday activity of making "communication possible between persons who are unable, for whatever reason, to communicate with each other directly" (Council of Europe, 2001, pp.87-88). Unfortunately, though, mediation was not developed to its full potential in the CEFR 2001. For example, there were no "can do" descriptors for this particular ability explaining what students could be expected to do at different proficiency levels. For this reason, mediation didn't have the same dramatic influence on the field of language teaching and learning as other parts of the CEFR 2001.

However, mediation did catch the eye of a small number of practitioners, who – perhaps not surprisingly given the increasing linguistic and cultural diversity in their society – found the potential of training students in cross-linguistic and cross-cultural mediation particularly exciting. Mediation quickly began to find its way into language classrooms throughout Europe. In Germany, for example, it started to appear in school curricula in the early 2000s. In Greece, on the other hand, mediation became a basic component of the KPG exam in 2003.

In 2014, the Council of Europe began developing a new set of "can do" descriptors for mediation. A provisional copy of the updated CEFR was released in 2018; the final version, in 2020. In addition to "can do" descriptors, this new *Companion Volume* to the CEFR offers a broader, richer conceptualisation of mediation. It moves beyond the focus on linguistic and cultural mediation in the CEFR 2001 to include mediation related to communication and learning. The authors of the CEFRCV state that this "wider approach has been taken because of its relevance in increasingly diverse classrooms [...] and because mediation is increasingly seen as a part of all learning, but especially of all language learning" (Council of Europe, 2020, p.36).

2 The CEFR

Before looking more carefully at how mediation is defined in the CEFR it would be useful to give a brief overview of the framework itself. The CEFR is a Council of Europe project whose aims are the following:

- promote and facilitate co-operation among educational institutions in different countries
- provide a sound basis for the mutual recognition of language qualifications
- assist learners, teachers, course designers, examining bodies and educational administrators to situate and co-operate their efforts

(Council of Europe, 2001, p.25).

With the goal of reaching these aims, the CEFR provides common reference levels for language competence from A1 (lowest) to C2 (highest), which are defined by illustrative descriptors provided in the form of "can do" statements. These are intended to promote a "proficiency perspective" rather than a "deficiency" one (2001, p.26), focusing on what learners *can* do, not what they *can't* do. Since the publication of the CEFR 2001, these common reference levels have permeated language learning and teaching in Europe and beyond, influencing the creation of countless objectives, targets and outcomes in this context (Figueras, 2012). In fact, it is common nowadays to refer to students as A1 or B2 instead of "beginner" or "upper intermediate."

One key concept of the CEFR is its vision of the user/learner as a *social agent* – that is, someone "acting in the social world and exerting agency in the learning process" (Council of Europe, 2020, p.22). For its authors, therefore, learning a language is not a passive experience but rather one involving personal engagement and active participation. This is particularly relevant to mediation, because, as a mediator, you are in a helping role. You are less concerned with your own opinions than with the communicative needs of the people around you. The mediator can provide this help in a variety of ways: "creating the space and conditions for communicating and/or learning, collaborating to construct new meaning, encouraging others to construct or understand new meaning, and passing on new information in an appropriate form" (Council of Europe, 2020, p.90).

With this idea of language learners as *social agents* at its core, the CEFR takes an "action-oriented approach" towards language learning and teaching. It does this by attempting to define an exhaustive list of all the possible kinds of *actions*, i.e. real-life tasks, language learners might perform with their languages, which are called *language activities* in the CEFR. These language activities are organised according to four *modes of communication* (production, reception, interaction and mediation), instead of the traditional four skills (reading, writing, listening and speaking), because, as the authors of the CEFR argue, this better captures the full nature of successful communication in the real world. Production, of course, includes speaking and writing; reception, listening and reading. Interaction, on the other hand, is a bit more complex. It involves both reception and production in a spoken or written dialogue—but, as we know, it is also more than a sum of those parts. Mediation goes one step further. Since it includes the process of developing and co-constructing new meanings, perspectives and ideas, this fourth mode involves reception, production and frequently even interaction. The chart below illustrates the relationship between the four modes.

Introduction

Figure 1: The four modes of communication (Council of Europe, 2020, p.34)

```
RECEPTION ─────────────────────────────────────→
         ╲       ╱                ╲
          ╲     ╱                  ╲
           ╲   ╱                    ╲
            ╲ ╱                      ╲
         INTERACTION ──────────→ MEDIATION
            ╱ ╲                    
           ╱   ╲                   
          ╱     ╲                  
PRODUCTION ←─────────────────────────────────────
```

In a podcast interview, Tim Goodier, one of the co-authors of the CEFRCV, explained the difference between interaction and mediation using the following metaphor:

> *If we see interaction like a game of tennis or ballroom dancing, then mediation is more like playing jazz. It's where you are doing two main things: interpreting the source of a text or something you've read or listened to and expressing it in your own way, and another is that the way you interact and collaborate with others creates something new.*
> (Wiseman, 2020, 1:58)

3 Types of mediation activities

As we have seen, the CEFRCV provides a compendium of language activities – that is, the real-life tasks language learners may need to perform using their languages. For mediation, these language activities are split into the following three macro groups: *Mediating a text*, *Mediating concepts* and *Mediating communication*. "We'll" start by discussing each of these macro groups individually and then we'll look at what they all have in common.

 **Mediating a text**

This type of mediation "involves passing on to another person the content of a text to which they do not have access, often because of linguistic, cultural, semantic or technical barriers" (Council of Europe, 2020, p. 91). Note that a *text* in this context could refer to a written, spoken, visual or multimodal text that contains some type of information or message, such as a magazine article, an oral presentation or conversation, a graph or infographic, or even a picture book. In this type of mediation, there is always both a *source text* – a text containing source information – and a *target text* – a new text created by the mediator through which they can pass on the source information to their target audience.

For *Mediating a text*, the CEFRCV (2020, pp. 92–108) defines the following language activities:

- **Relaying specific information** refers to the way some particular piece of information of immediate relevance is extracted from the source text and relayed to someone else.
- **Explaining data** refers to the transformation of visual information into a verbal text, such as figures found in graphs, diagrams, etc.
- **Processing text** involves understanding the information and/or arguments included in the source text and then transferring these to another text, usually in a more condensed form, in a way that is appropriate to the context.

Introduction

- **Translating a written text**[1] is the informal process of spontaneously giving a translation, in speech or in writing, of a written text, such as a notice, letter, e-mail or other communication.
- **Note-taking** concerns the ability to grasp key information and write coherent notes.
- **Expressing a personal response to creative texts (including literature)** focuses on expression of the effect that a work has on the user/learner as an individual.
- **Analysis and criticism of creative texts (including literature)** concerns more formal, intellectual reactions to creative texts.

Common activities that involve a degree of *Mediating a text* are information gap or jigsaw activities, peer or open class presentations involving a research phase, a film or book review, a report based on data, to name just a few.

Mediating concepts

Mediating concepts, on the other hand, "refers to the process of facilitating access to knowledge and concepts for others, particularly if they may be unable to access this directly on their own" (Council of Europe, 2020, p. 91). Parents, mentors and teachers will often find themselves in situations where they have to mediate concepts. However, the CEFR highlights that this type of mediation is also a key aspect of collaborative learning and work that produces new ideas and conclusions. In this context, everybody in the group may be acting as a mediator at some point during the task. In practice, this type of mediation overlaps to a degree with the principles behind the **Cooperative Learning** movement, which stresses the importance of positive interdependence and individual accountability in collaborative activities (Anderson, 2019).

For *Mediating concepts*, the CEFRCV (Council of Europe, 2020, pp. 108–113) breaks the types of mediation into two groups: collaborating in a group (constructing and elaborating meaning with others) and leading group work (creating the conditions for the exchange and development of new concepts):

- **Collaborating in a group**
  - **Facilitating collaborative interaction with peers** refers to when users/learners contribute to successful collaboration in a group that they belong to, usually with a specific shared objective or communicative task in mind. They are concerned with making conscious interventions where appropriate to orient the discussion, balance contributions and help to overcome communication difficulties within the group.
  - **Collaborating to construct meaning** is concerned with stimulating and developing ideas as a member of a group. It is particularly relevant to collaborative work in problem solving, brainstorming, concept development and project work.
- **Leading group work**
  - **Managing interaction** is intended for situations in which the user/learner has a designated lead role to organise communicative activity between members of a group or several groups, for example as a teacher, workshop facilitator, trainer or meeting chair. They have a conscious approach to managing phases of communication that may include both plenary communication with the whole group, and/or management of communication within and between sub-groups.

---

1. The CEFRCV only mentions written texts as source texts for this language activity. In this book, however, we've also included translating tasks with spoken and visual source texts. In our experience, there are times where you informally translate a spoken or visual text in much the same way you would a written one.

- **Encouraging conceptional talk** involves providing scaffolding to enable another person or persons to themselves construct a new concept, rather than passively following a lead. The user/learner may do this as a member of a group, taking temporarily the role of facilitator, or they may have the designated role of an expert (for example, an animator, teacher, trainer or manager) who is leading the group in order to help them understand concepts.

Typical classroom activities involving mediating concepts are those in which students are engaged in group work (for example to produce a poster or write a report), problem-solving tasks or group discussions with specific success criteria. However, the focus of the activity would be on the *process* of the group work rather than the *product*. To emphasise the mediation of concepts in groupwork, it helps if we assign specific roles or responsibilities to different members of the group (Goodier, 2020). If we put students (particularly younger learners) in a leading role during this sort of collaborative group work, we can help them develop leadership and other valuable life skills (Chiappini, 2020).

 Mediating communication

The third type of mediation, *Mediating communication*, "aims to facilitate understanding and shape successful communication between users/learners who may have individual, sociocultural, sociolinguistic or intellectual differences in standpoint" (Council of Europe, 2020, p. 91). A successful mediator in this context positively influences the interaction among all the participants. This is the type of mediation that is closest to people's traditional idea of mediation in the context of diplomacy or dispute resolution. However, the CEFRCV mainly focuses on how this type of mediation is used in everyday personal encounters, either social or professional. The CEFRCV (Council of Europe, 2020, pp.114–117) defines the following type of *Mediating communication*:

- **Facilitating pluricultural space** refers to the user/learner facilitating a positive interactive environment for successful communication between participants of different cultural backgrounds, including in multicultural contexts. It involves creating a shared space between linguistically and culturally different interlocutors (that is, the capacity to deal with "otherness", to identify similarities and differences, to build on known and unknown cultural features, and so on) in order to enable communication and collaboration.
- **Acting as an intermediary in informal situations (with friends and colleagues)** refers to situations where the user/learner acts as a plurilingual individual who mediates across languages and cultures to the best of their ability in an informal situation.
- **Facilitating communication in delicate situations and disagreements** involves the user/learner in a formal role to mediate in a disagreement between third parties, or in an informal one trying to resolve a misunderstanding, delicate situation or disagreement. The user/learner is primarily concerned with clarifying what the problem is and what the parties want, helping them understand each other's positions.

In the context of the classroom, it is interesting to note that the activities described above for *Mediating communication* are actually quite common but usually unplanned – that is, they are the result of inevitable conflict, disagreement or misunderstandings that occur while using a second language. To help students better cope with these situations, we can use roleplay or drama activities to give students low-stakes practice with the sort of high-stakes situations that await them outside of class (Chiappini & Mansur, 2020).

In the diagram below from the CEFRCV, you can see the complete list of the mediation activities described above. Note that in addition to mediation activities there are also mediation strategies, which will be discussed further in the micro-skills section.

Introduction

Figure 2: Mediation activities and strategies (Council of Europe, 2020, p.90)

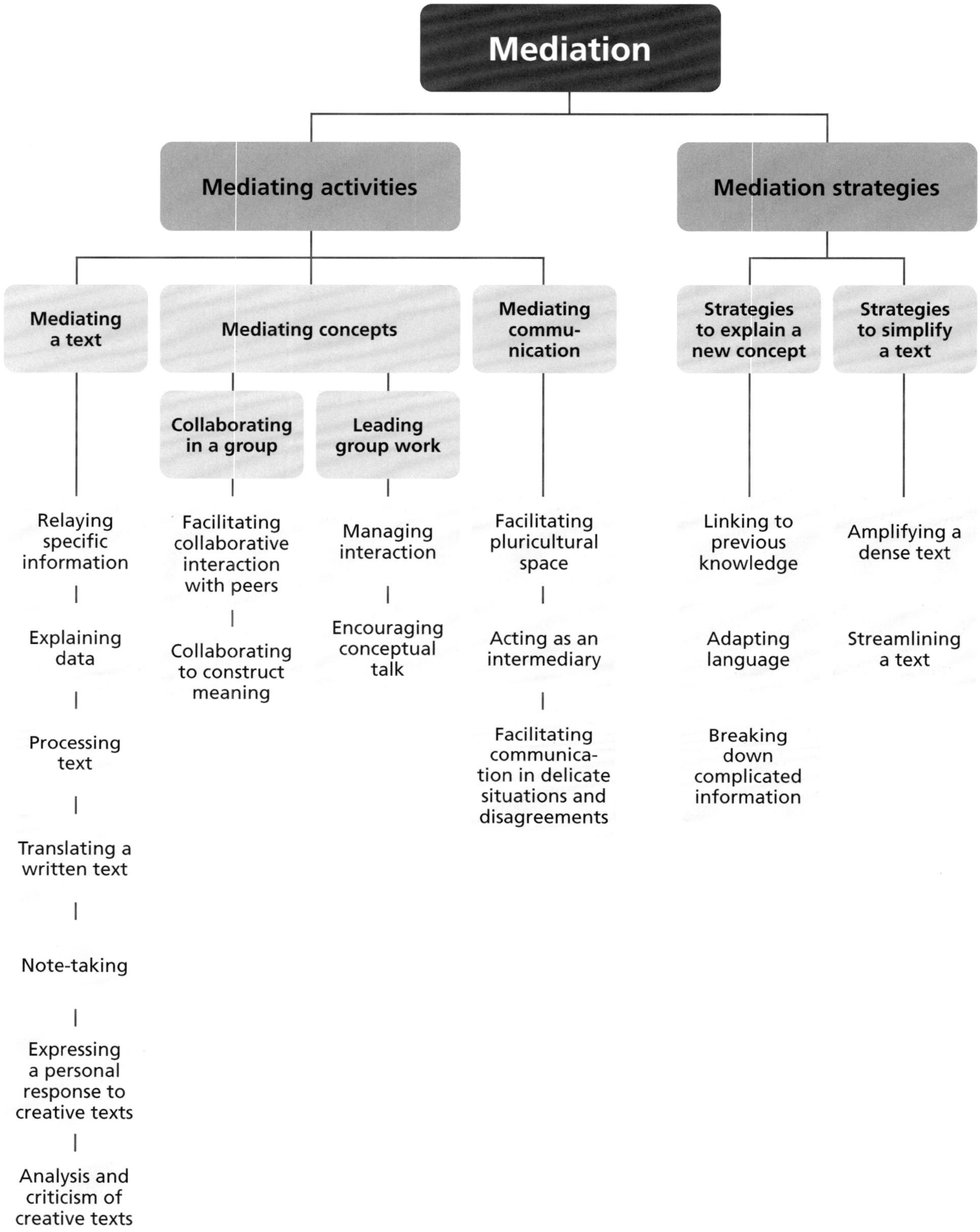

```
                                    Mediation
                    ┌───────────────────┴───────────────────┐
            Mediating activities                    Mediation strategies
      ┌───────────┼───────────┐                      ┌──────┴──────┐
  Mediating   Mediating    Mediating            Strategies      Strategies
   a text     concepts      commu-              to explain a    to simplify
              ┌───┴───┐     nication             new concept    a text
         Collaborating Leading
         in a group   group work
```

Mediating a text	Collaborating in a group	Leading group work	Mediating communication	Strategies to explain a new concept	Strategies to simplify a text
Relaying specific information	Facilitating collaborative interaction with peers	Managing interaction	Facilitating pluricultural space	Linking to previous knowledge	Amplifying a dense text
Explaining data	Collaborating to construct meaning	Encouraging conceptual talk	Acting as an intermediary	Adapting language	Streamlining a text
Processing text			Facilitating communication in delicate situations and disagreements	Breaking down complicated information	
Translating a written text					
Note-taking					
Expressing a personal response to creative texts					
Analysis and criticism of creative texts					

These three 'flavours" of mediation, as Goodier (2020) calls them, might seem quite different at first. In reality, though, they have a great deal in common. If you are in the role of a mediator in any of these activities, you will have to handle the communication of meanings and ideas, while at the same time taking into consideration the communicative needs of your audience, listener, reader or collaborators. As mentioned earlier, whether you are mediating a text, concepts or communication, you are in a helping role; you are less concerned with your own opinions or needs and you are more focused on successfully facilitating interaction, understanding or collaboration. In the words of Coste & Cavalli (2015, p. 15), "the aim of the mediation process, defined in the most general terms, is to reduce the gap between twopoles that are distant or in tension with each other." To do this, you will need a certain amount of emotional intelligence and empathy in order to understand the needs, viewpoints and even emotions of the people you are trying to help. It's also worth noting that in most mediation tasks you will find yourself using a group of common strategies, such as adapting language and summarising. Do refer to the micro-skills section for further discussion of these "mediation strategies".

As you can see in the diagram above, there are more language activities, and therefore more "can do" descriptors, for the macro group of *Mediating a text*, which is why this book contains a wider variety of tasks focused on this type of mediation. However, in practice, these three macro groups of mediation often overlap. So, even though we have designed each of the tasks in this book around one specific language activity, we found it natural to include more than one type of mediation within some of the tasks. For example, the pair or groupwork stages in a *Mediating a text* task often involve some degree of *Mediating communication* or *Mediating concepts*. Likewise, students may have to mediate texts as part of a task that is mainly focused on the mediation of concepts or communication.

4 Barriers to communication

In real life—or indeed in the classroom—the need for mediation often arises due to some kind of barrier to communication. These barriers might be linguistic, cultural, semantic or technical. However, it's important to note that a common barrier that gives rise to mediation is simply a lack of information. For example, we often find ourselves summarising the main events of a TV series that our listeners would be perfectly capable of watching themselves, but perhaps they simply haven't had the opportunity or time to do so. At times, we may even mediate in the absence of any kind of barrier to communication. This happens when we are articulating thoughts, often together with others, "groping towards a new understanding" (Piccardo et al, 2019).

5 Intralinguistic vs. cross-linguistic mediation

One fascinating thing about mediation is that it can be intralinguistic or cross-linguistic. In intralinguistic mediation, our students would be using source information and producing target texts in the same language (e.g. English). In cross-linguistic mediation, on the other hand, our students would be using source information in their L1 and mediate it in the target language (e.g. English). Take this B1 descriptor from the scales for *Relaying specific information* (Council of Europe, 2020, p. 94):

> Can relay (in Language B) the contents of detailed instructions or directions, provided these are clearly articulated (in Language A).

In this descriptor, Language A could be the student's L1 and Language B English. This type of cross-linguistic task would therefore, involve informal translation. However, there is a big difference between the type of translation in this activity and the work of professional interpreters and translators, who possess competences, both linguistic and technical, far beyond that of a typical language learner. Instead, the translation that occurs in a cross-linguistic mediation task consists of the kind commonly found in informal everyday situations among speakers of more than one language.

Another important difference between cross-linguistic mediation and translation is that, when in the role of the mediator, you are expected to put information into your own words. You are also expected to prioritise information. Depending on its relevance to the communicative needs of your target audience, as a mediator you not only *can* but are *expected to* add or leave out information, change the discourse, register or genre of the source text, etc. (Dendrinos, 2013). This is starkly different to professional translation, where the translator is expected to produce a new text that is as faithful to the original as possible.

There is one important point to make about how the descriptors for mediation in the CEFRCV are presented. According to the authors of the CEFRCV, "Language A" and "Language B" in the B1 descriptor above don't actually have to be different languages; they could also be varieties of the same language or different registers of the same language. In fact, they could also be identical with no linguistic barrier to overcome, because, as we have seen above, a simple lack of information is common context for mediation. Therefore, the B1 descriptor (Council of Europe, 2020, p. 94) above could be rewritten in the following way and still "count" as mediation:

> Can relay the contents of detailed instructions or directions, provided these are clearly articulated.

7 Challenges with cross-linguistic mediation

Using the L1 in class

If you have ever lived abroad and your friends or family came to visit you, the idea of cross-linguistic mediation will be very familiar to you. Perhaps you had to explain the contents of a menu or summarise a rental car agreement. If we think of our students as language *users* in addition to language *learners*, as the CEFRCV proposes, then it makes perfect sense to engage with this type of authentic context in the second language classroom – and therefore, to work with both English and the students' L1 in class. When you think about it, the use of the L1 in class opens the door to exciting possibilities of exploiting countless real-life situations involving cross-linguistic mediation that have so far been overlooked in the communicative language classroom.

However, we realise that some teachers might not be entirely comfortable using the students' L1 in class. For many teachers, the ideal English class is an English-only one, where the L1 is banned. Today the prevalence of "direct methods" and the idealisation of the native speaker as the best model for "proper" teaching still remain widespread in ELT. However, the use of L1 in class is no longer the "skeleton in the cupboard" (Deller & Rinvolucri, 2002, p.5) that it once was. Indeed, since the publication of Guy Cook's *Translation in Language Teaching* (2010), a consensus has grown in the academic community that a strategic, principled use of the L1 can in fact be quite beneficial to language learning. Given its real-life applications, cross-linguistic mediation is just this type of strategic, principled use of the L1.

What is more, if we acknowledge the L1 and put it to a useful purpose in class, we are showing respect for the students' mother tongue. Dendrinos (2006), for her part, sees the inclusion of mediation in the original CEFR 2001 as a sign of a growing positive attitude towards the idea of speaking more than one language. It also reflects the reality that our students (and we teachers) exist in a plurilingual space, where the ability to move from one language to another is completely natural and should be a source of pride. Indeed, for the Council of Europe, plurilingual and pluricultural competence are key aspects of the aims of language education (Piccardo et al., 2019).

Limited knowledge of the students' L1

Another challenge is that some teachers will have limited proficiency in their students' L1. They may fear that by engaging with the students' L1 in class they may risk exposing themselves to ridicule. This is obviously a legitimate concern. As we hope the tasks in this book illustrate, there is plenty that can be done to improve students' mediation skills with intralinguistic tasks — that is, tasks only involving English. However, if you are in this position and would like to use cross-linguistic tasks, a good crutch is to use texts that have already been professionally translated, such as the sort of brochures available at the tourism office in your town or city. You could use the English version as a cheat sheet when checking to see if students have left out any important information in the L1 text. Though it may be intimidating, one benefit of using cross-linguistic tasks for teachers with limited knowledge of their students' L1 is that it promotes an understanding of the language learning process and creates a sense of "comradeship, the feeling of being on a shared journey" (Chiappini & Mansur, 2020).

Multilingual groups

One last challenge to address when working with cross-linguistic mediation tasks is to what extent this is possible with multilingual groups, where students don't share an L1 or understand each other's L1s. This context certainly limits the types of possible cross-linguistic tasks. However, you could still have students do mediation tasks where, for example, they research a topic in their L1 and then transmit this information in English to their classmates. This type of mediation activity allows students the opportunity to share aspects of their pluricultural identity that might never come to the surface in a strictly "English only" learning context.

1 Mediation strategies

As described in the CEFRCV, mediation strategies are used by the mediator to "clarify meaning and facilitate understanding" (Council of Europe, 2020, p. 117). Many of these strategies will be familiar to teachers as "communication" strategies. However, the authors of the CEFRCV have included them within this language mode and have called them "mediation" strategies because, as we will see in more detail in this section, they come in particularly handy to language users – and therefore our students – when they need to mediate texts, concepts and communication.

To make these strategies more accessible to teachers, however, we have adapted the list from the CEFRCV mentioned in the introduction, adding in a few more based on our experience teaching mediation. In each of the mediation activities in the book, we have included a section where you will find the most important strategies that your students need to use to complete them. You can use this list as a reference as you read through the book:

1. Selecting and omitting information
2. Summarising
3. Paraphrasing
4. Translating
5. Transforming visual information into verbal text
6. Linking to previous knowledge
7. Explaining
8. Combining
9. Expanding
10. Adapting language
11. Breaking down complicated information
12. Explaining sociolinguistic and sociocultural elements

Strategies and tips for scaffolding

As we have said above, mediation strategies aren't only relevant to mediation. These are indeed communication strategies that our students might already be using when doing language activities related to the other language modes (i.e. reception, production and interaction). Some of our students will obviously find some of these communication strategies easier or just more natural to use. However, all of them will certainly benefit from further training in mediation strategies. As Dendrinos (2013) observes when talking about mediation strategies and candidates' performance in mediation tasks in the Greek national exams (KPG), "it is important to stress that with training and coaching, foreign language learners and exam candidates are bound to have better results, as with all types of other language practices". Scaffolding these valuable strategies in the ELT classroom, then, seems to be a good path to follow to help students become more successful mediators.

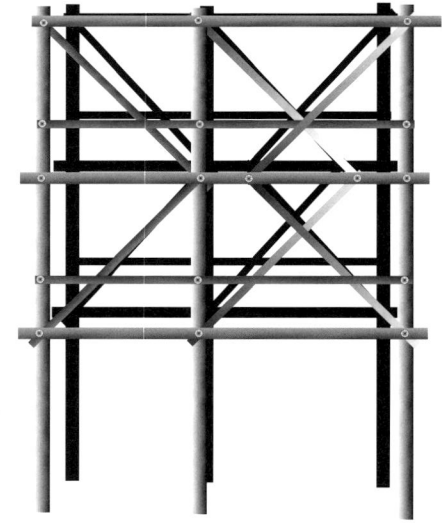

In the following section, we are going to explain each mediation strategy and give you ideas on how you can scaffold each one of them in your mediation lessons.

1 Mediation strategies

1 Selecting and omitting information

Before mediating (i.e. before "producing a target text", "talking ideas through" while collaborating in group work, or "moderating" communication), students in the role of the mediator may need to tackle one or a series of source texts – that is, read written texts, listen to spoken texts or interpret visual data – in order to identify meanings. Students will then have to sift through these meanings to select only the information that is relevant to the target situation and context.

To provide our students with specific training for this strategy, we should first guide them to discover where key information is found in written texts (e.g. relation between topic sentence and supporting ideas in paragraphs), spoken texts (e.g. intonation) and visual data (e.g. relation between numbers, texts and images). Then, in preparation for a mediation task, we can ask our older or higher-level students to find the key points in the source text and then underline or summarise them in a short list in their notebooks. Our younger or lower-level students, on the other hand, may find it easier to choose the key point or points from a given list of options that we will have carefully prepared beforehand. Another constructive way of raising students' awareness of how to select and omit information is to give them the opportunity to reflect on what makes information relevant or not. Once they have identified the key points in a text, we can lead an open-class discussion of these, where students can share their ideas and give reasons why they selected certain ones and omitted others.

2 Summarising

Summarising or *streamlining* a text basically means giving a short account of its main points. Our students might need to summarise source information to pass on the main points contained in a text (*Mediating a text*), to give a rundown of what has been said during a discussion and decide on the next step to take (*Mediating concepts*), or to quickly sum up the key issues in a debate (*Mediating communication*).

To train our students in this strategy, we could ask our younger or lower-level students to read or listen to a source text – or a shorter section of it – and then choose the most appropriate summary from a list of options, which could be individual sentences or longer summaries. With older or higher-level students, we could ask them to identify a limited number of keywords in the source text and then use these to write a sentence or a shorter text that summarises it. Another way to train our students to streamline texts could be to provide them with a gapped written summary of a text they have just read, and ask them to fill it in with keywords. The level of difficulty will certainly depend on the topic as well as the lexis and the structures present in the text. This activity would not only provide students with training in identifying the main ideas in a text, but it would also provide them with a model of a good summary, helping them notice key elements such as the choice of key points that are relayed, the order in which the ideas are developed, the length and so on.

3 Paraphrasing

If summarising may imply reusing the same keywords that students have identified in a source text or selecting and communicating main ideas, paraphrasing means using words and language that are different from the source text in order to relay the same message or information contained there.

Our older or higher-level students might be better able to handle sentence transformation exercises, which provide effective training in paraphrasing. We could also help them learn how to use the dictionary or thesaurus more effectively, for example by focusing their attention on the different levels of register or frequency of a lexical item or grammatical structure. Our younger or lower-level students, on the other hand, might benefit from doing activities that include more guidance, such as answering multiple-choice questions to choose the correct or most appropriate synonym or synonymical expression for a given word, structure or sentence. Another way to help improve our students' paraphrasing skills could be having them focus on lexical chains, helping them notice how skilled writers and speakers use synonyms, antonyms, hyponyms and so on to develop the same idea or ideas throughout a text. Once students have identified a specific or multiple lexical chain, we could ask them to use the individual items to rewrite the original text, for example, or even produce a similar text of their own on the same topic. Finally, as a follow-up activity, we should also encourage them to record new items in the lexical chains in their notebooks or on their phones, making lists, spidergrams, card sets and so on (Chiappini, 2021).

4 Translating

As Tim Goodier (2020) reminds us, "informal translation is a part of the mediation scales, but it's not about developing translation skills". Mediators, in fact, aren't professional translators. More than working towards "replicating" a text using another language, they rather prioritise information, leaving out irrelevant points on purpose or even adding extra information or context. This is something that a professional translator, on the other hand, wouldn't normally do. When translating informally, in fact, students as mediators will have to identify key information in a source text in one language (i.e. usually their L1), and then relay this in a different language (i.e. the target language), to a new target audience and through a new text (i.e. target text).

To train our students to informally translate for cross-linguistic mediation tasks, we could create multiple-choice activities with different options of translation into English of a particular sentence, section or whole text written or spoken in the students' L1. Our younger or lower-level students could be presented with simpler concepts, shorter sentences or smaller chunks of language. Our older or higher-level students, instead, might be able to analyse more challenging shades of meaning or levels of register, for example by presenting them with different options of translations that could be all correct, but only one of which matches a specific situation or context in which mediation is required.

5 Transforming visual data into verbal texts

In order to mediate visual data successfully, students need to be able to 'read' the different types of graphs, that is, understand the meaning or aim of the figures shown. They will also have to know how to explain these data in words, for example in a presentation or report, and how to do so in an organised way.

To train our students to better interpret visual information, we could present them with appropriate graphs and infographics, encouraging them to look at the data to deduce possible first conclusions and then summarise these in a few sentences. To train our students to lay out a target text in which they have to explain visual data, we could first present them with good models of oral or written descriptions of graphs and infographics – such as oral presentations or written reports – and then invite them to analyse how the information has been logically structured by the speaker or writer. Finally, we could encourage them to work out some useful tips they have worked out from analysing the models, such as how to organise their description (e.g. Step 1: *Introduce the graph/s.* Step 2: *Give an overview of the content of the graph.* Step 3: *Explain the relevant details. …*), etc.

1 Mediation strategies

6 Linking to previous knowledge

To better activate our reader's or interlocutor's schemata and, therefore, help them better understand the information we are going to relay, we can first of all consider and or elicit what our target audience already knows about the topic.

To train our students to become better at this strategy, we can give them a word or concept for them to explain in peer presentations. We could first ask them to find examples from their audience's previous knowledge – i.e. considering their cultural background, daily life experiences, etc. – that they think could help them explain the word or concept more effectively. We could then ask them to include these examples in their peer presentations. This activity could include a reflection stage where students consider to what degree using the strategy of linking to previous knowledge came in useful or not. Another idea is to make it a requirement in student presentations that speakers ask their audience a few questions at the start to help them understand how much the audience actually knows about the topic they are going to present. In this case, we can give our younger or lower-level students a list of model questions like the ones below, to choose for their own presentation.

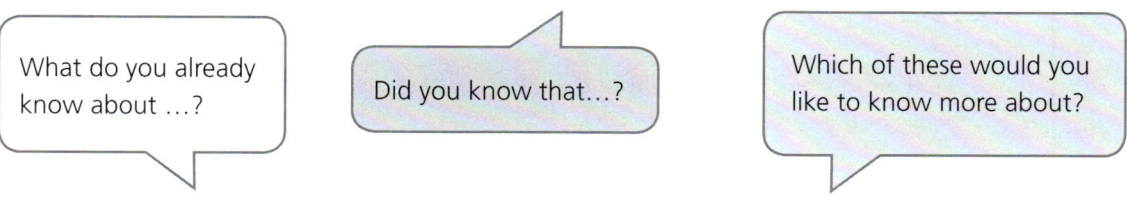

As for our older or higher level students, we could include a pre-task discussion phase where students try to get a feel for how much their audience (the class) already knows about their topic and then encourage students to create more questions to elicit more information if necessary.

7 Explaining

As we saw at the beginning of the chapter, the overall objective of using mediation strategies is to clarify, therefore to "explain" information. In the activities and throughout this book, however, we will consider "explaining" as a separate strategy, or better, a separate set of strategies that include exemplifying, defining and comparing.

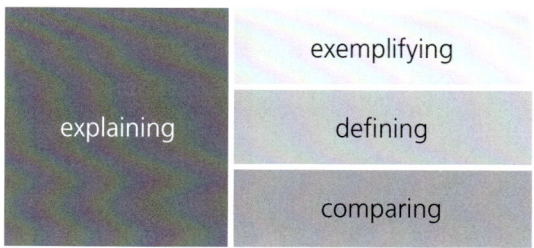

Before a mediation task we can always pre-teach our students useful language for them to exemplify, define and compare. But to scaffold these micro-strategies more appropriately, we can always go the extra mile and present our students with model texts in which skilled writers or speakers "use" language to give examples, definitions and make analogies. We could first guide our students to discover the words, phrases and expressions from the model texts and then offer them the opportunity to practise these in short speaking activities to explain concepts and opinions.

1 Mediation strategies

8 Combining

When relaying information from a text, students will inevitably need to combine:

1) different pieces of information from the same text or different texts
2) information from the source text with relevant extra-textual information (e.g. personal or shared background knowledge and experiences)

It goes without saying that for students to successfully combine information, they will need to know how to link ideas logically in a way that produces the desired effect in the audience. Therefore, a focus on conjunctions and other linking devices will be paramount, followed by activities in which students take different keywords or key concepts from different sections of a text or from different texts, and then summarise them in a logically and appropriately structured way. After that, students can also reflect on how well they have done this during peer or open-class feedback.

9 Expanding

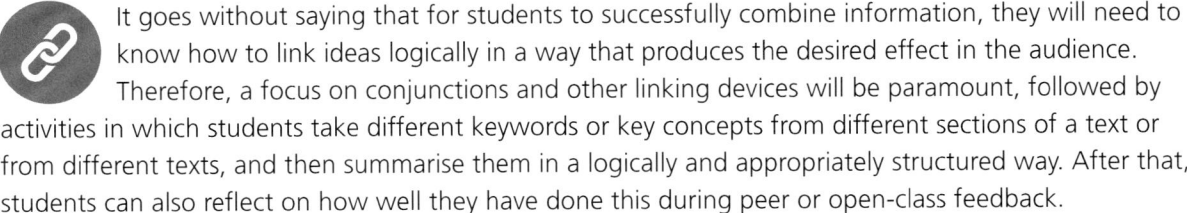

With the goal of making a text more accessible to a specific target audience, students may need to expand information by making a text more detailed or descriptive. This can be done by adding more concrete examples, alternative points of view, definitions, analogies and so on.

When our students are preparing for a writing task or a presentation, we could encourage them to read again what they have written in their drafts or notes, and while they do so, ask themselves "how" and "why" questions. The objective would be for them to check whether there is more to say about each of the points they have made, or if the ideas they would like to use in their target text could be broken down into two or more parts and developed further separately instead.

Another effective way to train our students to expand on information in target texts could be using chain-type activities: we could divide our class in small groups and give each group a different definition (e.g. of a particular object or concept). Students then write a short text in which they expand on the definition by adding extra information such as examples, analogies, further definitions, etc. in order to make it easier to understand. After that, we could ask groups to swap texts and ask them to further expand on what the other group has produced by changing or adding more examples, analogies and comparisons themselves. Finally, students could also discuss the positive elements of each of the texts they have produced, commenting on which text better expands on a particular piece of information or concept.

10 Adapting language

In a mediation task, students have to produce a target text that is often of a different genre, register and style from the source text. For example, students may be asked to read an extract from a specialised text (e.g. a clause in a tenancy agreement) and adapt it for a younger or less specialised audience who isn't familiar with the topic or vocabulary in the text and therefore can't understand it on their own (e.g. first-year university students renting a flat for the first time). To simplify information, our students will of course need to be able to paraphrase, summarise and explain, but they will also have to "adjust their delivery", that is, use grammar, vocabulary, register, style and so on that are appropriate to their target audience.

To train our students to adapt language, we could present them with a specialised text – i.e. a text that is about a specific topic that contains specific, technical vocabulary – and then ask them to relay the key information from it in a peer or open-class presentation. While students prepare, we could first encourage them to think about what words or concepts the other students might have trouble understanding. We could then give them time to think about which synonyms, examples and/or extra definitions they could use to bridge the knowledge gap between the audience and the text. We could present our older or higher-level students with more specialised texts and then ask them to turn these into magazine articles or text messages to friends. With our younger or lower level students, we can also use texts about technical topics, but the data or language in these texts will obviously have to be within their range and level. For example, we could ask them to watch a video showing someone making a simple dish and have them take notes on the various steps in the process. They could then practise explaining to a friend how to make the dish.

11   Breaking down complicated information

As the authors of the CEFRCV explain, breaking down complicated information means splitting it 'into its constituent parts and [then showing] how these parts fit together to give the whole picture' (Council of Europe, 2020, p. 118). This may involve:

- sequencing information in a way that is more accessible to the target audience
- describing a process, ideas or instructions as a series of steps or bullet points

In order to simplify a text, students will need practice not only in summarising, paraphrasing, explaining and adapting language, but they will also need to know how to relay information in an appropriate, logical sequence. This means that, before relaying key information from a source text, we shouldn't only ask our students to classify it as "major/minor", or "relevant/irrelevant", but also think about how to organise it in a suitable way, e.g. in a chronological or thematic order, keeping in mind the audience's familiarity with the topic. Conferencing activities, such as group and open-class discussions in which students reflect and share their ideas on how to organise complex information, are a particularly good starting point for training our students in this mediation strategy. A more specific example of scaffolding activity, though, could be presenting students with different versions of how key information from a source text could be sequenced and asking them to choose which one might be more appropriate for a specific target audience (e.g. a younger and less experienced audience, someone more familiar with the topic).

12   Explaining sociocultural elements

Whether we are meditating texts, concepts or communication, there may be certain sociocultural cues related to a specific culture or discourse community (e.g. meal or public transport conventions) that may need extra explanation in order to be understood – and not be misunderstood.

To successfully explain sociocultural elements, students in the role of the mediator will need to be familiar with both their own and the target culture. Students will therefore need enough exposure to cultural content of and from the cultures they need to mediate between (Chiappini, 2020). We could present students with written, audio or video materials that include concepts, ideas or views that are specific to their own or the target culture and ask them to identify the specific elements that someone unfamiliar with this culture would find hard to understand. Students could then think of how best to explain these sociocultural cues. Younger or lower-level students, for example, could focus on simpler aspects, such as the way people greet each other, the different times they have a meal during the day, or how people spend their free time. They could watch a video showing how children their age from the target culture do any of

1 Mediation strategies

these everyday activities, and answer comprehension questions as they watch it – or we can stop the video ourselves and guide them with appropriate concept checking questions. Our older and higher-level students, on the other hand, could be challenged with more specific or more controversial topics, such as cultural misunderstandings and stereotypes. For example, we could ask them to watch a scene from a movie showing a situation of communication breakdown because of a cultural misunderstanding. Then, in pairs or small groups, we can ask them to reflect on how the misunderstanding could have been avoided, or even act out the same scene but this time including a mediator, who moderates the situation and helps avoid or repair the misunderstanding.

Competences

On top of specific mediation strategies, students will also need to be trained to evaluate the elements that make up the different situations in which mediation is required, and obviously how to perform in them. These elements are:

- the **target audience**, i.e. who they are, what they already know about the topic, etc.
- the **communicative purpose**, i.e. why the target audience want or need the information, why they don't have access to it, etc.
- the **conditions and constraints of the communicative context**, i.e. format, style and therefore genre of the target text through which the information is relayed

This then means that students as mediators also need to be provided with opportunities to develop and refine the following competences:

- **sociolinguistic competence**, e.g. recognising and using appropriate polite forms and more general communication conventions; mediating information through an appropriate register; recognising sociocultural and cross-cultural cues (Council of Europe, 2020, p.136)
- **pragmatic competence**, i.e. organising spoken or written discourse (i.e. genre knowledge); logically presenting ideas in a text and show how they relate to each other (Council of Europe, 2020, p. 137)
- **plurilingual and pluricultural competence**: being aware of similarities and differences between cultures; using cultural elements neutrally and critically to improve communication (Council of Europe, 2020, p. 123)

All these strategies and competences make language users/learners not only better at mediating, but also and more importantly, better **social agents** who collaborate and co-construct meaning to understand, explain and find new solutions.

Further considerations for training

1. **When to scaffold strategies** – Scaffolding can happen either before or after students have completed, or have attempted to complete, a mediation activity. The advantage of doing mediation training before an activity is that, since mediation has only recently started to appear in coursebooks, students (and teachers) may not be familiar with the format of a mediation task. Training in mediation strategies will naturally help familiarise students with what they will need to do in this sort of task. The advantage of scaffolding relevant strategies after a task, on the other hand, would be for students to have a better chance to reflect on their performance and understand what they have done well and what they may need to work on more.

2. **Language** – Mediation tasks don't lend themselves particularly well to language practice. Based on our experience of teaching mediation, a focus-on-form stage is most useful after the students have completed a mediation task, even more so if the students haven't been able to complete a task

1 Mediation strategies

successfully because of some language gap. That said, especially at lower levels of linguistic competence, we have found it useful to pre-teach key vocabulary and useful expressions that will help students better carry out a particular task. This allows students to focus on the mediation task at hand and not get tripped up when they don't have all the language they need.

3 **Task repetition** – Research has shown that task repetition leads to better fluency and more language complexity. Bygate (2009) suggests this might be because students already have "experience" of the task. According to him, in fact, this helps students build on their previous performance and therefore do better the second time around. Although research on mediation is still quite scarce, based on our experience teaching mediation in the ELT classroom, students act as much more confident mediators the second time they attempt to complete a mediation task, reusing strategies and language more fluently and naturally.

4 **Strategies and mediation macro groups** – The different types of strategies required by the students to complete a mediation task will necessarily depend on the type of mediation activity they need to perform (Stathopoulou, 2015). For example, to mediate data (i.e. mediating a text), students will necessarily need to explain, break down complicated information and combine intra-textual information (i.e. the data from the source graph or series of graphs) with extra-textual information (i.e. the audience's previous knowledge of the topic, its beliefs, etc.). To mediate concepts or communication, on the other hand, both students will need to explain, paraphrase, summarise and combine information while collaborating. For this, and as we will also see in more detail in **How to create tasks and adapt materials**, it's important to think about which strategies our students will need to complete a particular task, and then decide how much support or training they will need before doing the task.

5 **Modelling mediation** – For students to have a clear idea of what they are meant to do, especially at the beginning of the mediation training, it's important to provide them with models. We can model an activity ourselves by showing students, for example, how in a cross-linguistic mediation task involving texts, the source information in the students' L1 is not reported literally but rather processed and summarised in the target language. Or we could even temporarily take on the role of leader or moderator in a concept or communication tasks ourselves, showing how the information needs to be passed around, explained, summarised and combined, so that groups and parties can reach a solution in a problem-solving task, or come to an agreement in a debate.

6 **CEFR descriptors** – It goes without saying that we can sensitise our students to each different type of mediation strategy and activity by using the very same descriptors from the CEFRCV. We could select some descriptors that are relevant to the strategy or set of strategies we want to teach in one class; simplify the language in them as necessary to make them more accessible to our students; and finally create scaffolding materials and activities out of our selection of descriptors. For example, we could create card games in which students match strategies and description of a situation in which the strategy is being used, or we could print the descriptors as simple lists and then analyse the meaning of each descriptor together with our students in open class, etc. (Goodier, 2020)

2 Mediating a text

2.1a B is for bureaucracy

 About the activity

Mediation task type	Relaying specific information in speech
Mediation strategies	Paraphrasing, translating, explaining, breaking down complicated information
Summary of the activity	Students roleplay a situation where a student explains to a foreign couple how to complete an important bureaucratic process that they would find difficult to understand on their own.

Rationale

Bureaucracy can be frustrating to deal with in our own countries, but it is a great deal more intimidating abroad, where we are less familiar with the language and we have to deal with official documents and processes. So it is very useful, even necessary, at times to have the help of a local in this type of situation.

 How to run the activity

Levels	B1–B2	Learners	Teens/Adults	Time	45 minutes

Preparation	- Make enough copies of the worksheet so that each member of the class will have a card. Cut up the cards. - Do some research online and fill out the information in the cards for health insurance, national identity card and residency. This will provide you with an answer key to assist and assess the students during the task. - Make sure students have access to the internet using their mobile phones or tablets.
Procedure	1. Lead into the topic by showing the students a picture of a young couple. Scan the DELTA Augmented symbol to find some pictures you can use. Explain that they are from a foreign country and are coming to work or study in the students' country. They speak English relatively well, but they still only have a limited grasp of the local language. Elicit some ideas from the class about what these young people might find difficult at first, e.g. finding a place to live, sorting out important documents, etc. Explain that this couple is feeling a bit overwhelmed with the bureaucracy in your country. They have asked you for help specifically with applying for health insurance and a national identity card, as well as establishing residency.

2.1a B is for bureaucracy

Procedure	2. Organise the students into small groups of three. Assign each group a bureaucratic process to research and hand out the cards. Encourage them not to limit their searches to the official information on government websites in their L1 but also to look at other sources, such as blogs, where the information may be presented more simply with foreigners in mind. 3. Once the groups have filled out their cards with all the necessary information, ask them to spend some time rehearsing how to explain the process in the most simple, straightforward way possible. 4. Regroup the students into groups of threes. Each group should have a student who has researched a different bureaucratic process. 5. The students then take turns roleplaying the situation. Students in the role of the foreign couple take notes and then double-check the information is correct by repeating it back to the student in the role of the local. Encourage the 'foreign couple' to pretend not to understand things at times and ask for clarification or the definition of certain difficult vocabulary, etc. 6. Give feedback in open class to round off the activity.

Language	– Lexis related to bureaucracy: *form, apply for, fill out, make a photocopy*
	– Modals of obligation: *You mustn't forget…, You'll have to arrange an appointment first, You need to make three photocopies of…*
	– Functional language for:
	  • Asking for clarification: *I'm not sure what you mean by… What is…? Sorry, I didn't quite get the last bit about…*
	  • Describing a process: *First you have to… Once you have… Finally…*
	  • Giving directions: *To get there, you have to take line 6 to… The address is …*
	  • Giving advice: *If I were you, I'd… Remember… Whatever you do, don't forget to…*

▼▲ Differentiation	– If the students have a hard time getting started during the research stage, you could give them suggestions on good sites to start looking for information. – During the rehearsal stage, some students may have difficulty simplifying the process into a reasonably short explanation. They may describe the process in far too much detail. In this case, encourage the other students in the same group to identify information that might be left out or summarised.

2.1a B is for bureaucracy

Variation and extension	- For multilingual groups, students could be grouped by nationality or work individually for the first stage where they research the bureaucratic processes. They could then do the roleplay stage in groups with students from other nationalities. - Students could also do the research at home before the lesson, then rehearse and perform the roleplay in class. - This activity lends itself well to task repetition. After having students reflect on their first attempt at the roleplay, regroup them and they can give it another go.
Feedback	This should focus on how well the students are able to explain the process in a way that a foreigner could understand, while not omitting any important details. You should also offer feedback on how they handle requests for clarification by their classmates. In a peer-feedback stage following the roleplay, students could reflect on how confident they would feel if they had to go through these bureaucratic processes themselves in real life.
Adaptation for the virtual classroom	Introduce the task in the main room and then put the students into breakout rooms to do the roleplays. Instead of cards, you could send the students the appropriate worksheet in the form of a PDF via the chat box (or by email before the lesson starts). During the research stage, students could work in a shared document to pool their notes.

2.1a B is for bureaucracy – the worksheet

RESIDENCY

What forms do you need to fill out?

Can any or all the process be done online? If so, how?

If you can't apply online, what office do you need to go to? Where is it and how do you get there?

Do you need to make an appointment? If so, how?

Do you need to present any specific documents? If so, which ones? Original/photocopy?

Are there any fees? If so, how and how much do you have to pay?

Is there anything else important that you need to know about this process?

2.1a B is for bureaucracy – the worksheet

NATIONAL IDENTITY CARD

What forms do you need to fill out?

Can any or all the process be done online? If so, how?

If you can't apply online, what office do you need to go to? Where is it and how do you get there?

Do you need to make an appointment? If so, how?

Do you need to present any specific documents? If so, which ones? Original/photocopy?

Are there any fees? If so, how and how much do you have to pay?

Is there anything else important that you need to know about this process?

2.1a B is for bureaucracy – the worksheet

HEALTH INSURANCE

What forms do you need to fill out?

....

....

Can any or all the process be done online? If so, how?

....

....

If you can't apply online, what office do you need to go to? Where is it and how do you get there?

....

....

Do you need to make an appointment? If so, how?

....

....

Do you need to present any specific documents? If so, which ones? Original/photocopy?

....

....

Are there any fees? If so, how and how much do you have to pay?

....

....

Is there anything else important that you need to know about this process?

....

....

2.1b Debunked!

 About the activity

Mediation task type	Relaying specific information in writing
Mediation strategies	Selecting and omitting information, summarising, paraphrasing, adapting language
Summary of the activity	Students research fake news on social media and write a brief post "debunking" it.
Materials	• Copies of at least five examples of social media posts containing "fake news" • Digital devices • Access to the internet • 2.1b Debunked! – the worksheet

Rationale

This activity helps students develop media information literacy as well as their ability to select and relay the most important and/or relevant pieces of information from a number of sources.

 How to run the activity

| Levels | B2–C1 | | Learners | Teens/Adults | | Time | 45–60 minutes |

Preparation	– Find at least five examples of social media posts containing misinformation or "fake news." There are a number of websites where you can find fake news from social media, such as the "Reality check" section of the BBC website (www.bbc.com/news/reality_check), www.factcheck.org, www.snopes.com, www.politifact.com, among others. Print out enough copies of these examples for students to look at in pairs. – Make sure at least half the students have mobile phones or tablets with access to the internet.
Procedure	1. Lead into the activity by asking students if they think fake news on social media is a problem in their country. Ask them where they would look for more information if they wanted to check the accuracy of a particular post. 2. Organise the students into pairs. Explain Activity 1, in which students work together to rank the reliability of various sources of information. Remind them there are no correct answers; the goal is to reflect on the quality of information in these sources. Hand out a copy of the worksheet to each student. Elicit or provide the meaning of *reliable*. 3. Regroup the students into new pairs. Ask them to compare their lists and report on how they decided the order with their previous partner.

2.1b Debunked!

Procedure	4. In open class, display one or two examples of fake news from social media. Elicit what makes the posts suspect or obviously unreliable. Depending on the example, you might point to some of the following: • The sources are not credible (or none are provided). • Little or no evidence is given (or the evidence seems unreliable/exaggerated). • The post is written to create "shock value," i.e. evoke an emotional response (fear, anger, excitement). • Images appear to be altered. • The story has not been reported in any mainstream media. • Using common sense, the story just doesn't "sound right". 5. Hand out more examples of fake news from social media. In their pairs, students do Activity 2. Briefly feedback in open class. 6. Tell students they are now going to do web-based research on one of the posts and then write a new post for social media "debunking" the fake news. Give them a moment to choose individually. Then regroup students according to which post they have selected. Explain that the students can do the web-based research in English, their L1 or any other languages they know. Remind them to include the information in bullet points. 7. Circulate and provide support as necessary while the students do Activity 3. 8. When finished, students attach their posts to the walls of the classroom with adhesive putty. Everyone walks around the room and reads their classmates' posts. Then, as a group, students vote on which group debunked their fake news most convincingly. 9. Give feedback on the task.
Language	– Lexis related to the topic of fake news: *spread false information, exaggerated, completely inaccurate* – Reported speech: *The original post claims that…, My partner said…* – Passives: *The post was reshared 34 thousand times, No sources were provided.* – Functional language for: • Referring to a source: *According to the WHO website…, In an article in The New York Times… One study shows…*
▼▲ Differentiation	– Some students might benefit from a model of the target text, i.e. a social media post debunking a fake news story. You could create one based on the information that accompanies each of the fake news stories which appear on the fact-checking websites listed in the preparation section. – An alternative way of leading into the lesson would be to tell a brief story about how you were personally taken in by a fake news story and inadvertently help spread it. If you strike a humble note at the beginning, it will help you to avoid sounding patronising and get the students "on board" for the rest of the lesson.

2.1b Debunked!

Variation and extension	– For monolingual groups, if you share or are familiar with the students' first language, you could find examples of fake news on social media in their L1, which the students would then discuss and debunk in English. – Students could collaborate on the research part of stage 7, but write their new posts debunking the fake news individually. – After the lesson, you could put the students' posts on a real social media platform, perhaps using the school's social media account, so the posts could be reshared, liked, etc.
Feedback	This should focus on how well students are able to find and then concisely summarise the information collected from different sources. Questions to guide your feedback on the task could include: • *Have the students selected good quality information from a variety of reliable sources?* • *Have they included links or references to their sources?* • *Have they used an appropriate register?* • *Is the post clear and easy to read?*
Adaptation for the virtual classroom	The example social media posts from stage 5 could be saved as a PDF and sent to the students via email or the chat box. Pair and group work could be done in breakout rooms. You could set up Activity 1 on the worksheet as a poll, with students ranking each from 1–5 (1 unreliable, 5 very reliable). At the end of the lesson, students could take turns using the screen sharing function to share their posts.

2.1b Debunked! – the worksheet

1 Work in pairs. Rank the following sources of information from most reliable (1) to least reliable (8).

- [ ] A YouTube video
- [ ] An article in an online newspaper
- [ ] A post on social media
- [ ] An article from an academic journal
- [ ] A book
- [ ] An entry on Wikipedia
- [ ] An official government website
- [ ] An official website for an international organisation

2.1b Debunked! – the worksheet

2 Work in pairs. Your teacher will give you some examples of fake news posted on social media. What makes the posts seem suspect or obviously unreliable?

3 Work in groups. Choose one of the posts from Activity 2 and write a new post for social media in which you:

- Explain what information in the original post is inaccurate or untrue.

- Provide a summary of more accurate information you found about the topic or story.

- Include links or references to reliable sources of information.

 Like    Comment    Share

   Write a message...

2.1c Flat hunting

 About the activity

Mediation task type	Relaying specific information in speech
Mediation strategies	Selecting and omitting information, translating, explaining sociocultural elements
Summary of the activity	Students help somebody who doesn't speak the local language find and decide on rental accommodation.

Rationale

Deciding where to live in a new place is difficult and it can be particularly stressful if you are unfamiliar with the local language. So it can be very useful to have a local who is willing to help you.

 How to run the activity

Levels	A2–B1	Learners	Teens/Adults	Time	30 minutes

Preparation	Go on a website that lists rooms, flats and houses for rent in the students' hometown or city, for example, www.idealista.com for Spain, Italy and Portugal. Find six listings in the students' L1 that might be suitable for the people in the role cards and print them out.
Procedure	1. Lead into the topic by asking students what the best way would be to find a room, flat or house to rent in their city or town. 2. Explain the situation: a visitor who does not know the local language is coming to live in your city or town for six months. They have asked for your help finding a room, flat or house to rent. You find a number of listings of available accommodation on a website, but they only appear in the local language. 3. Assign roles. Give the adverts to the students in role of the mediator. Students in the role of the foreign visitors each get one of role cards 1–3. 4. Allow students time to prepare. In small groups, students in the role of the mediator look at the adverts and discuss the best way to describe the rental accommodations in English. Students in the role of the visitor, who are also in small groups, fill out their role cards and discuss what kind of accommodation they are looking for and why.
Procedure	5. Put the students into pairs, with one student in the role of the mediator and the other in the role of the visitor. They perform the roleplay. Explain that there is only a very limited number of accommodations available and that students in the role of the visitor must choose one from the available options. 6. Give feedback on the task in open class.

2.1c Flat hunting

Language	- Lexis to describe flats, room or houses: *balcony, blinds, furnished, in the outskirts*
	- Modals of obligation and prohibition: *You can't use the bathroom downstairs, You must put down a deposit.*
	- Functional language for:
	  - Describing accommodation: *It's got high ceilings, There's one available parking space.*
	  - Expressing preferences: *I like rooms with…, I'd prefer a place that is…*
	  - Expressing rules: *Smoking is not allowed, It says no loud music after 11 p.m.*
	  - Making recommendations: *This one seems like a good fit because… If I were you, I'd go with this one because…*

▼▲ Differentiation	- If you think some of your students might struggle to describe accommodation in English, you could pre-teach certain keywords or lexical phrases. - Some students might find the spontaneous nature of roleplays challenging. To reduce the stress of having to think on the spot, they could write out their dialogues and then perform them. - To make the task more challenging, instead of finding examples of possible accommodation yourself, ask the students in the role of the mediator to use the search function on the website to find suitable rental accommodation.
Variation and extension	- You could ask students to find adverts in their L1 and email them to you before the lesson, so you can print them out. - For multilingual classes, the adverts could be in English. If mobile phones or tablets are allowed, you could provide the students in the role of the mediator with a list of the links to available accommodations and they could look at the listings on their phones.
Feedback	This should focus on how well the students in the role of the mediator select and relay key information from the adverts, and how well they explain it to their classmates. After finishing the task, students could discuss the following questions: - How well was the mediator able to explain the information in the rental listing? - Was the explanation clear and easy to follow? - Was there anything that needed further explanation? - What made the task challenging? Why? Were you able to overcome these challenges? - Do you think you could do this in real life? Why or why not?
Adaptation for the virtual classroom	Instead of roleplay, this activity could be done via email with the teacher copied in. The students in the role of a visitor could send the first email, explaining that they need help finding a place to live and what they are looking for. Students in the role of the mediator could respond with a link to available rental accommodation and a short description of the rooms, flats or houses. The email correspondence could then continue with students asking and answering specific questions about the accommodation.

2.1c Flat hunting – the cards

Card A

You work for multinational company. It's important for you to learn the local language for work, so your company has paid for you to do a six-month intensive language course. You are looking for accommodation.

Complete the following information:
- How much you can pay in rent ....
- Kind of accommodation you are looking for (room, flat, house) ....
- Preferred location ....
- Preferred amenities (lift, back garden, washing machine, etc.) ....
- Other preferences ....

© DELTA Publishing, 2021 | www.deltapublishing.co.uk
ISBN 978-3-12-501744-3

ACTIVITIES FOR MEDIATION
by Riccardo Chiappini and Ethan Mansur

Card B

You have recently finished your university degree in an English-speaking country. You will be working as a language assistant at a local secondary school. You are looking for accommodation.

Complete the following information:
- How much you can pay in rent ....
- Kind of accommodation you are looking for (room, flat, house) ....
- Preferred location ....
- Preferred amenities (lift, back garden, washing machine, etc.) ....
- Other preferences ....

© DELTA Publishing, 2021 | www.deltapublishing.co.uk
ISBN 978-3-12-501744-3

ACTIVITIES FOR MEDIATION
by Riccardo Chiappini and Ethan Mansur

Card C

You are a seasonal worker who has been given a six-month work visa. You will be employed by a local farm. You are looking for accommodation.

Complete the following information:
- How much you can pay in rent ....
- Kind of accommodation you are looking for (room, flat, house) ....
- Preferred location ....
- Preferred amenities (lift, back garden, washing machine, etc.) ....
- Other preferences ....

© DELTA Publishing, 2021 | www.deltapublishing.co.uk
ISBN 978-3-12-501744-3

ACTIVITIES FOR MEDIATION
by Riccardo Chiappini and Ethan Mansur

2.1d Giving and following instructions

 About the activity

Mediation task type	Relaying specific information in speech
Mediation strategies	Selecting and omitting information, summarising and/or expanding, paraphrasing, breaking down complicated information
Summary of the activity	Students listen to, take notes on and relay contents of detailed instructions or procedures.

Rationale

Giving and receiving instructions/procedures is an activity that takes place in everyday interaction, not only within the occupational and educational domains, but also within the public and private domains. If we focus on how to mediate know-hows 'of all shapes and sizes', therefore, we can provide students with the opportunity to reflect more carefully on how to use language not only to explain the content of a set of instructions, but also to best adapt this to their partners' knowledge, linguistic and sociocultural background.

 How to run the activity

| Levels | B1–B2 | Learners | Primary/Teens/Adults | Time | 60 minutes |

Preparation	- Print worksheet below – one copy for each of your students. - As a backup, bring in source material yourself: e.g. written lists of instructions downloaded from the internet, video links to tutorials (if phones, tablets or computers available), etc.
Procedure	1. Lead into the topic by asking students to think about a set of instructions or a procedure they know how to follow and that they would be able to give to other students in class: e.g. *how to edit photos on a phone, how to make brownies*, etc. In case students have trouble finding something appropriate to use, see the Preparation section above. 2. Organise the class into pairs. Students tell each other what set of instructions or procedure they know about and why they know about it. 3. Assign roles: Students A and B. Hand out the worksheet to both As and Bs. Ask them to fill in the INSTRUCTIONS TO GIVE section. 4. Students A gives instructions to Students B, who take notes in the INSTRUCTIONS TO LEARN section. Encourage As to speak at normal speed and Bs to take notes only of the key points instead of trying to note down everything. Bs can ask As clarifying questions either during A's explanation or at the end. 5. Bs repeat their summarised version of the procedure/instructions back to As. As check that all the information has passed on successfully and either repeats and/or clarifies points as necessary.

2.1d Giving and following instructions

Procedure	6. Reverse roles. 7. Students give each other feedback on task (e.g. considering how clear the explanation was, whether anything important was left out, if and how their partners clarified their doubts, etc.). 8. Give feedback on task.

Language	- Sequencers: *after that/afterwards, as soon as, before, first, next, then*
	- Phrasal verbs connected with technology and DIY: *back up, drag to/into, go offline, put back, screw in/out, take off/out*
	- Lexis will vary depending on topic/subject of the instructions chosen to relay
	- Functional language to
	  • ask for clarification – *Am I on the right track?, Could you remind me what…?, Could you say that again, please?*, etc.
	  • provide extra information and advice: *'Always/Never…', 'Be careful (not) to…', 'It helps if…', 'Remember to…'*

▼▲ Differentiation	Less confident and lower-level students could prepare for the task in advance: they could either watch a YouTube tutorial, for example, or read a text provided by the teacher.
Variation and extension	- In a plenary, students can share what they have learnt to do in class thanks to their partners and vote for the most useful/interesting ones. - As homework, teachers could ask students to record their instructions either as voice memos or vocal messages, for example, and send them to all the other students to listen to and learn, as well as the teacher for them to give further/more thorough feedback. - In groups, students are encouraged to reflect on their performance and how useful they have found the activity. At lower levels, students could answer questions such as *How useful did you find this activity? Which parts did you find easier/more difficult? Why?* Whereas, at higher levels, students can be given more freedom to discuss what went particularly well and what they feel they need to improve.
Feedback	This should focus on how well the students have relayed and understood the instructions. Some questions that teachers could ask themselves while monitoring may be: - *How effectively have students used the mediation strategies appropriate for this task?* - *Have they taken into consideration their interlocutor's background knowledge?* - *How did they respond to their partners' requests for clarification?* - *Were they able to accurately retell the instructions received from their partner(s)?*
Adaptation for the virtual classroom	Students could do stages 3–6 in breakout rooms. Also, instead of relaying the instructions to each other, students could make a video or audio tutorial themselves and share it with the class or post it on a video or audio platform that allows posting and sharing (YouTube and SoundCloud, for example).

2.1d Giving and following instructions – the worksheet

INSTRUCTIONS TO GIVE:	INSTRUCTIONS TO LEARN:
Objective: *(e.g. converting YouTube videos into mp4 or mp3 files)*	Objective: *(e.g. converting YouTube videos into mp4 or mp3 files)*
•	• ....
Steps:	Steps:
•	• ....
•	• ....
•	• ....
•	• ....
•	• ....
•	• ....
•	• ....
Difficult points to explain:	Difficult points to explain:
•	• ....
•	• ....
•	• ....

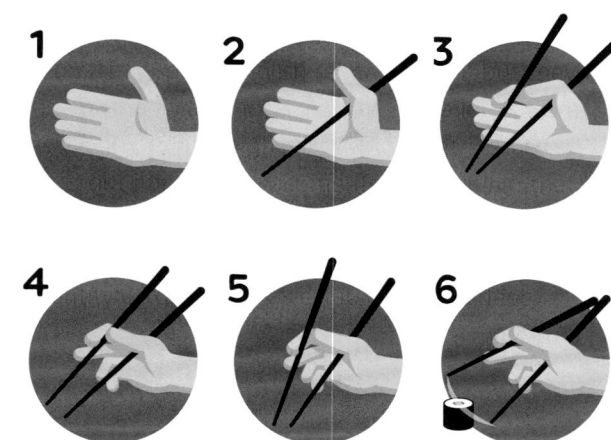

2.1e Multilingual media*

About the activity

Mediation task type	Relaying specific information
Mediation strategies	Selecting and omitting information, paraphrasing, translating, explaining
Summary of the activity	Students compare a news story written in their first language to a different version written in English.

Rationale

This task encourages students to evaluate differences in the way news is reported, focusing on which information is included or excluded, as well how much importance is placed on particular aspects of the story in different versions.

How to run the activity

Levels	B2–C1	**Learners**	Teens/Adults	**Time**	45 minutes

Preparation	Find a relatively short news story (one or two pages) written in English about a topic or event that will also have been reported on internationally. Then find two versions of the same news story in the students' L1. Make a copy of the English version for all the students and enough copies of the L1 versions for half the class to read each one of the articles.
Procedure	1. Lead into the activity by showing the students the headline of the news story in English. Elicit what they know about this particular story. If they are unfamiliar with it, provide a brief summary. 2. Explain the task: Before reading the news story in English, students will read two different versions of the same news story in their L1. 3. Hand out a copy of the worksheet to each student. Give half the students one version of the news story and a different version to the other half. Tell them to take notes on the questions in Activity 1 while they read the news articles. 4. Organise the class into pairs. Students compare their answers. 5. Tell students they are now going to read the same news story in English and answer the questions in Activity 2 individually. This activity encourages students to reflect on differences between the two versions. 6. Put the students into small groups. They discuss their answers to the questions in Activity 2. Circulate and provide support as necessary.

* The inspiration for this activity came from one by Jason Anderson called "Translingual jigsaw" in Activities for Cooperative Learning.

2.1e Multilingual media

Procedure	7. Round off the activity with an open class discussion of the most interesting differences the students found. 8. Give feedback on the task.

Language	- Lexis related to the media: *sensationalise, bias, sources*
	- Lexis related to the topic of the specific news story (for example, a hurricane): *blow down, blackout, torrential rain*
	- Passives: *The coastline was completely destroyed…, Thousands were left homeless.*
	- Past perfect: *The storm had ripped through Guatemala and Honduras before it hit Nicaragua*
	- Functional language to
	  • Referring to the source text: *In the article I read, it says…, According to the English version…*
	  • Comparing: *In this article…, while in the other one I read, it says…, The English version focuses more on…*
	  • Hypothesising: *They might have placed more importance on X because…, Maybe they thought readers wouldn't be familiar with…*

▼▲ Differentiation	- Consider your students' interests and level when selecting a news story. Avoid topics that you think would be too controversial or divisive in your teaching context, as well as any news stories your students might find upsetting for one reason or another. - To add extra challenge, you could ask students to consider differences in style, e.g. the average length of sentences or paragraphs. You could also discuss possible issues of bias or underlying assumptions.
Variation and extension	- One variation could be reading different versions of an obituary of a famous person who recently passed away. - In multilingual groups, students could read different English language versions of the same story from different types of newspapers, for example, one version from a broadsheet and another from a tabloid.
Feedback	This should focus on how well students have been able to select relevant information from both the article in their L1 and the English version, and then incorporate it into a group interaction. Questions to guide your feedback could include: - *Did the students succeed in identifying and discussing similarities and differences between the English version and the versions in their L1?* - *How well did the students use appropriate mediation strategies, such as translating, paraphrasing and explaining?*
Adaptation for the virtual classroom	You could put students into breakout rooms during the pair and group work stages; the open class activities could be done in the main room. While discussing the articles in breakout rooms, students could use the screen sharing function to highlight certain sections or details in order to make comparisons.

2.1e Multilingual media

1. You are going to read a news story in English. But first, you are going to read a version of the same news story in your first language. Take notes on the following questions.

   a. What happens in the story?
   b. What makes this story interesting and "newsworthy"?
   c. If there are images, what do they tell you about the story?
   d. How many sources are referred to in the story?
   e. Your teacher will give you an English version of this story later. What differences do you think there might be between the two versions?

2. Work in pairs. Discuss your answers to the questions in Activity 1.

3. Now read the English version of the news story. Take notes on the following questions.

   a. Does one of the versions focus more on a particular aspect of the story?
   b. Is there any information that is not included in one version of the story but appears in another version?
   c. In English, the more important the information is, the closer it is to the beginning of a news article. Is the order of information the same or different in the different versions?
   d. If images are used, are there any differences in the type of image chosen?
   e. Does one version of the news story include fewer sources than another? In general, do the sources seem reliable?
   f. Can you think of any explanations for the differences you found?

4. Work in small groups. Discuss your answers to the questions in Activity 3.

2.1f Nail your essay!

💡 About the activity

Mediation task type	Relaying specific information in speech
Mediation strategies	Selecting and omitting information, summarising, paraphrasing, explaining
Summary of the activity	Students listen to part of a seminar on how to write good essays and then summarise the most relevant points in a short audio message to a friend who needs help improving her own essay.

Rationale

Tips on how to write good essays are certainly useful for students and teachers alike, both in the short and long term. But knowing how to select and omit information from a dense text and make it accessible to someone who needs it, is a skill that is transferable to many other contexts. When we can't do something well, either because we might have missed a lesson, training course or talk, it's always good to have someone else step in and lend us a hand.

▶ How to run the activity

Levels	B2–C1	Learners	Teens/Adults	Time	45 minutes

Preparation	– Make a copy of the **Worksheet** and **Peer-feedback form** below for each of your students. – Make sure at least half of your students have a voice recording application on their phone (most phones have it inbuilt) and that they have access to the internet from the classroom.
Procedure	1. Lead into the topic by asking students to work in pairs and discuss the following questions: • *What do you do when you have to write an essay?* • *Do you find it easy or difficult?* • *What tips would you give to someone who finds essay writing challenging?* 2. Encourage students to share their ideas with the rest of the class. 3. Give a copy of the worksheet to each of your students. Ask them to read the essay and answer questions 1–3 in Activity 1. Then, invite students to compare their ideas in open class. **Note:** At this stage, you shouldn't reveal too many positive or negative points yourself, otherwise your students would be left with no mediation to do in the next stages.

2.1f Nail your essay!

Procedure	4. Tell students to read the rubric in Activity 2. Ask them questions to check understanding. 5. Students listen to the seminar and take notes. 6. Organise the class into new pairs. Ask pairs to compare their notes and agree on the ones they should include in their voice message. Monitor and assist as necessary. 7. Now ask pairs to record their voice message using a voice recording app or a text message application like WhatsApp on their phones. (Suggested length of voice message: 3 minutes). Monitor and assist as necessary. **Note:** Remind students that before sharing their voice message, they should double-check that their voice messages contain all the points they selected in the previous stage. 8. Explain the peer-feedback stage: ask pairs to swap their voice messages with another pair, for example, via WhatsApp, email or Bluetooth. Ask them to listen to the recording they have just received and use the questions in the peer-feedback form to prepare to comment on it. 9. Give a copy of the peer-feedback form to each of your students. Pairs swap recordings and prepare to give feedback using the peer-feedback form. Monitor and assist as necessary. 10. Pairs give each other feedback using the peer-feedback form. 11. Now, encourage pairs to record their voice messages again including some of the tips they exchanged during the feedback stage. 12. Give feedback on task.

Language	- Lexis to talk about essay writing: *argument, counterargument, evaluate, layout/lay out*
	- Modals of deduction: *have to, need to, must, should*
	- Functional language to
	  • paraphrase: *Basically…, In other words…, To put it another way…, What I mean is (that)…*
	  • give advice: *Always/Never…, Be careful (not) to…, Be sure to…, It helps if…, It's important to…, Remember to…*

▼▲ Differentiation	Some students might find the listening challenging. Provide them with the transcript to make sure they have enough points to include in their voice message.
Variation and extension	- Written mediation: instead of an audio message, students could write an email or a text message. - Students could use the same procedure to focus on other types of texts, such as articles, reports and reviews, for example. For this, find suitable videos or audio recordings with tips on how to write the text type you've chosen and use these instead.

2.1f Nail your essay!

Feedback	This should focus on how well the students have understood and relayed the content of the original text and the rationale behind their choices. On top of the suggested answer key (below), here are some more questions you could answer while monitoring might be: 1. Did students select and include the relevant tips? 2. How clearly did they summarise and explain these? 3. Did they leave out any key points from the source text? 4. Was the students' voice message organised and easy to understand? Suggested answer key for task (in same order as in the audio): **Relevant tips from seminar** 1. <u>Some information is not relevant:</u> Make sure you include enough relevant information for each of the points provided in the instructions. 2. <u>Opinion is not clear until the very conclusion:</u> Make sure your stance is clear right from the start / avoid revealing your opinion only at the end of the essay. 3. <u>Information in paragraphs is disorganised and difficult to follow:</u> Avoid long sentences with too many conjunctions and other linking words. 4. <u>No title:</u> Use the question from the instructions or invent one yourself! **Other tips** 5. <u>Plan your essay:</u> Decide what your key points are and write them either in the form of notes or complete sentences. 6. <u>Proofread it or have it proofread by someone else:</u> Confirm that the facts and examples are correct and make sure that there are no spelling mistakes! 7. <u>Use topic sentences:</u> Describe the point you want to make in the first sentence of a paragraph. Then, in the sentences that follow, give more details and examples that support the point you've made in the first sentence.
 Adaptation for the virtual classroom	– Use the chat box to share the worksheet and the peer-feedback form. – Stages 5, 6, 8 and 9 can be done in breakout rooms.

2.1f Nail your essay! – the worksheet

Activity 1

Read the essay below and…
1. choose a suitable title.
2. comment on both positive and negative aspects of the essay.
3. decide whether the essay is okay or if you think it needs editing.

> Is getting into higher education better than leaving school to work?
> Write your essay using the following notes:
> Write about:
> - *Work experience*
> - *Salary prospects*
> - *(Your idea)*

> There are both advantages and disadvantages to getting into higher education after school.
>
> Those who opt for a degree might have more time to decide what job to do later on in life. Another advantage might be that they can get more qualifications and therefore more chances to get a more satisfying and better-paid job than people who start work after school, and what's more, higher education gives people the opportunity to join different clubs and socialise with the people they might have more in common with.
>
> Going to work straight after school, on the other hand, might also mean missing out on the chance to start earning money, while students at university might need more time to be able to pay their student loan back to the bank and another disadvantage is that people who spend time studying won't have much left for them to also gain work experience and build their CV. This will make it even more challenging for them to get a foot on the career ladder.
>
> In conclusion, every year, millions of school leavers have to face with the dilemma whether to start a degree or a professional career. Some of them might feel or even be responsible enough for such a decision. Others, on the other hand, might need more support through this decision-making process. I believe that going into Higher Education is anyway the better path to take. Although higher education students might not be able to build their CV while studying, at the end of their degree, they will definitely help them climb the career ladder faster than those who will have chosen a career path instead.

Activity 2

Your friend has just sent you an essay she has written. She says she isn't happy with it and would like you to help her. She asks you to read her essay and send her a voice message with some tips on how she could improve it.

Listen to part of a seminar in which senior lecturer, Beatrice Anelli, gives tips on how to write a good essay. In your notebook, take notes of the tips that can help your friend improve her essay.

2.1f Nail your essay! – the essay answers

…

There are both advantages and disadvantages to getting into higher education after school.

Those who opt for a degree might have more time to decide what job to do later on in life. Another advantage might be that they can get more qualifications and therefore more chances to get a more satisfying and better-paid job than people who start work after school, and what's more, higher education gives people the opportunity to join different clubs and socialise with the people they might have more in common with.

Going to work straight after school, on the other hand, might also mean missing out on the chance to start earning money, while students at university might need more time to be able to pay their student loan back to the bank and another disadvantage is that people who spend time studying won't have much left for them to also gain work experience and build their CV. This will make it even more challenging for them to get a foot on the career ladder.

In conclusion, every year, millions of school leavers have to face with the dilemma whether to start a degree or a professional career. Some of them might feel or even be responsible enough for such a decision. Others, on the other hand, might need more support through this decision-making process. I believe that going into Higher Education is anyway the better path to take. Although higher education students might not be able to build their CV while studying, at the end of their degree, they will definitely help them climb the career ladder faster than those who will have chosen a career path instead.

Problem 4:
No title.

Problem 2:
no clear line of argument from the start (also see comment in "conclusion")

Problem 3:
information is disorganised – long sentences with too many conjunctions or linking words, etc.

Problem 1:
irrelevant information – "(Your idea)" piece of information is irrelevant and not explained.

Problem 3:
information is disorganised – long sentences with too many conjunctions or linking words, etc.

Problem 2:
line of argument only revealed at the end.

2.1f Nail your essay! – the peer-feedback form

Activity 3

With a partner, use your notes to agree on which tips from the seminar you would like to pass on to your friend. Then, together, summarise the tips and record your voice message for your friend.

1. Peer-feedback form

Listen to the voice message recorded by another pair and answer the following questions. Use the column on the right to note down your answers.

Questions	Your answers
1. Do you think the voice message is too long or too short?	
2. Do you think it includes appropriate tips for your friend?	
3. Do you think the tips are easy to understand and follow?	
4. Are there any points that the other pair should explain better? Which?	
5. What do you like about the voice message?	
6. If any, what recommendations would you make for the other pair to improve their voice message?	

2.1g Travel advice

About the activity

Mediation task type	Relaying specific information
Mediation strategies	Selecting and omitting information, translating, explaining sociocultural elements
Summary of the activity	Students watch a video in their L1 about a holiday destination in their home country. They then write an email to an English-speaking friend, giving them advice on what there is to do and see there.

Rationale

When planning a trip abroad, it's not always easy to find information in your L1 about holiday destinations, particularly lesser-known ones. In this case, it's very useful to have a friend who knows the local language who can help you access information in a language you don't understand.

How to run the activity

Levels	B1–B2	Learners	Teens/Adults	Time	45–60 minutes

Preparation	– Find a short video (no longer than five minutes) in the students' L1 that gives information about a holiday destination in their country. Ideally, it should be about a place that students may have heard of but will probably be less familiar with, for example, trying "base" in the Hardanger fjord in Norway. – Think of some background information about the English-speaking friend: they are outdoorsy, like to cycle, don't like spicy food, etc. (Note that it's not necessary for the friend to be from an English-speaking country, as English is widely used as a lingua franca.) By providing this information, you will help train students in the valuable mediation strategy of selecting and passing on only the most appropriate information from a source text, instead of simply relaying a list of everything mentioned. – Make a list of relevant information in the video that students would be expected to pass on to their English-speaking friend.
Procedure	1. Lead into the activity by asking students what they usually do when they want to find information about a holiday destination in a foreign country. 2. Introduce the context and the English-speaking friend using a photo and a short description – who they are, what they like to do, if they like to travel on a budget, etc. Explain that the background information about the friend will be important when deciding what information to select from the video.

2.1g Travel advice

Procedure	3. Students watch the video and take notes on what the English-speaking friend could see and do in the holiday destination. They then compare notes in pairs. 4. In open class, elicit some of the students' ideas. Explain that there may be some sociocultural elements that might need extra explanation to someone with little or no familiarity with the local culture, food, geography, etc. Elicit a few examples and brainstorm ways to explain them, for example, *There's a traditional dish from the region that you really must try. It's called …… and it's made from…* Or *Remember that people eat dinner a bit earlier here.* 5. Individually, students write their emails, which they then swap with another student when finished. They read each other's emails and respond with a short thank-you note, a couple of follow-up questions, etc. 6. Give feedback on the task.
Language	- Giving advice: *You can't miss…, It's probably best to avoid…* - Explaining sociocultural elements: *Have you heard of …? It's a type of… In this city, it's traditional for people to…* - Expressions for informal emails: *Hi (friend's name), Good to hear from you. Let me know if you need any more help.* - Lexis related to the holiday destination (for example, visiting a fjord): *cliff, narrow, shallow*
▼▲ Differentiation	- If you think the students will find the writing stage challenging, put them into pairs and have them write and respond to the emails together. - If needed, you could familiarise the students with the genre of informal letters before the writing stage, perhaps with a list of informal expressions and linkers, common opening and closing formulas, etc. - This task could be made more difficult by choosing a video about a place that would be harder to describe in English.
Variation and extension	For multilingual groups, students could find their own short video in their L1 about a holiday destination in their home country, but remind them that it should be a place they are not very familiar with. Instead of writing an email to a friend, students could show a short clip of the video to their classmates and then give the group advice about travelling to this place. Or they could create a short video of themselves giving their tips and play it for the class. Their classmates ask follow-up questions.
Feedback	This should focus on how well the students were able to identify and pass on only the most relevant information from the source text, as well as how well students followed the conventions of an informal email.
Adaptation for the virtual classroom	You could show students the video in the main room using the screen sharing function. Students then write their emails during or after the lesson and then send it to another classmate with the teacher cc'd in.

2.2a Gaming galore

 About the activity

Mediation task type	Explaining data in writing
Mediation strategies	Selecting and omitting information, transforming visual information into verbal text, explaining, combining
Summary of the activity	Students select data from an infographic about playing video games and include these in an essay for a magazine.

Rationale

This task provides students with the opportunity to practise useful mediation skills at the same time as they also develop their essay writing skills.

 How to run the activity

Levels	C1–C2	Learners	Teens/Adults	Time	90 minutes

Preparation	Make a copy of the worksheet for each of your students.
Procedure	1. Organise the class into pairs. Ask pairs to discuss and make predictions about the following points: • countries with most videogame players • average videogame player profile (age and sex) • advantages and disadvantages of playing video games 2. Give a copy of the worksheet to each of your students. Ask pairs to read the information in the infographic in Activity 1 to check their predictions from stage 1. 3. Explain mediation task: students use relevant information in the infographic to write an essay (150–200 words) on the topic of video games. They will plan their essay in class, but they will write it at home. 4. Ask students to read the essay question in their worksheet and check understanding. Then students do Activity 2, which asks them to select the information from the infographic that they think they will need in order to better answer the essay question. Monitor and assist as necessary. 5. Organise the class into pairs. With their partners, students plan their essays discussing the guiding questions in Activity 3. Monitor and assist as necessary. 6. In open class, encourage students to share their plans and answer any of their questions.

Procedure	7. Set a deadline for students to complete and hand in their essays. 8. Once you receive them, prepare to give feedback on task.

Language	– Lexis to talk about research on video games/the video game industry: *addiction, arcade, developer, shooter*
	– Passive voice and other impersonal constructions: *Playing video games is believed to increase…, The graph shows that most gamers are…*
	– Functional language to
	  • express result: *Since only a small number of users have been reported to seek professional help, then…, As a result of playing video games, a person can develop…*
	  • contrast information: *Although there have been a few cases of…, The benefits, on the other hand…*
	  • explain trends: *In the past five years, there has been an increase/decrease in…, A high number of gamers have been reported to…*

▼▲ Differentiation	Some students might not be familiar with the features of the genre: choose a model essay that is appropriate for your students/course objectives (e.g. a narrative essay for General English students, argumentative for EAP, etc.) and have them analyse it before they do the task.
Variation and extension	This task could be made cross-linguistic by having students analyse data where the information is shown in their L1. Find charts, graphs, infographics on the internet or make your own using PowerPoint, Keynote or similar applications.
Feedback	This should focus on how well the students have answered the essay question using the data from the infographic. Some questions that you could answer while and after monitoring might be: – *Have they used relevant points from the infographic to answer the essay question?* – *How well have they explained these?* – *How well have they combined their opinion and their selection of data from the infographic?* – *How relevant are the examples provided to support their opinion?* – *Is the style appropriate?*
Adaptation for the virtual classroom	– (Stage 4). Share your screen to show the essay question and then send your students into their breakout rooms to plan their essay. – (Stage 6) Students plan their essay using a shared online document. Ask them to share the document with you right from the start as this will make your monitoring easier.

2.2a Gaming galore – the worksheet (Page 1/2)

Activity 1

Look at the infographic and check your predictions.

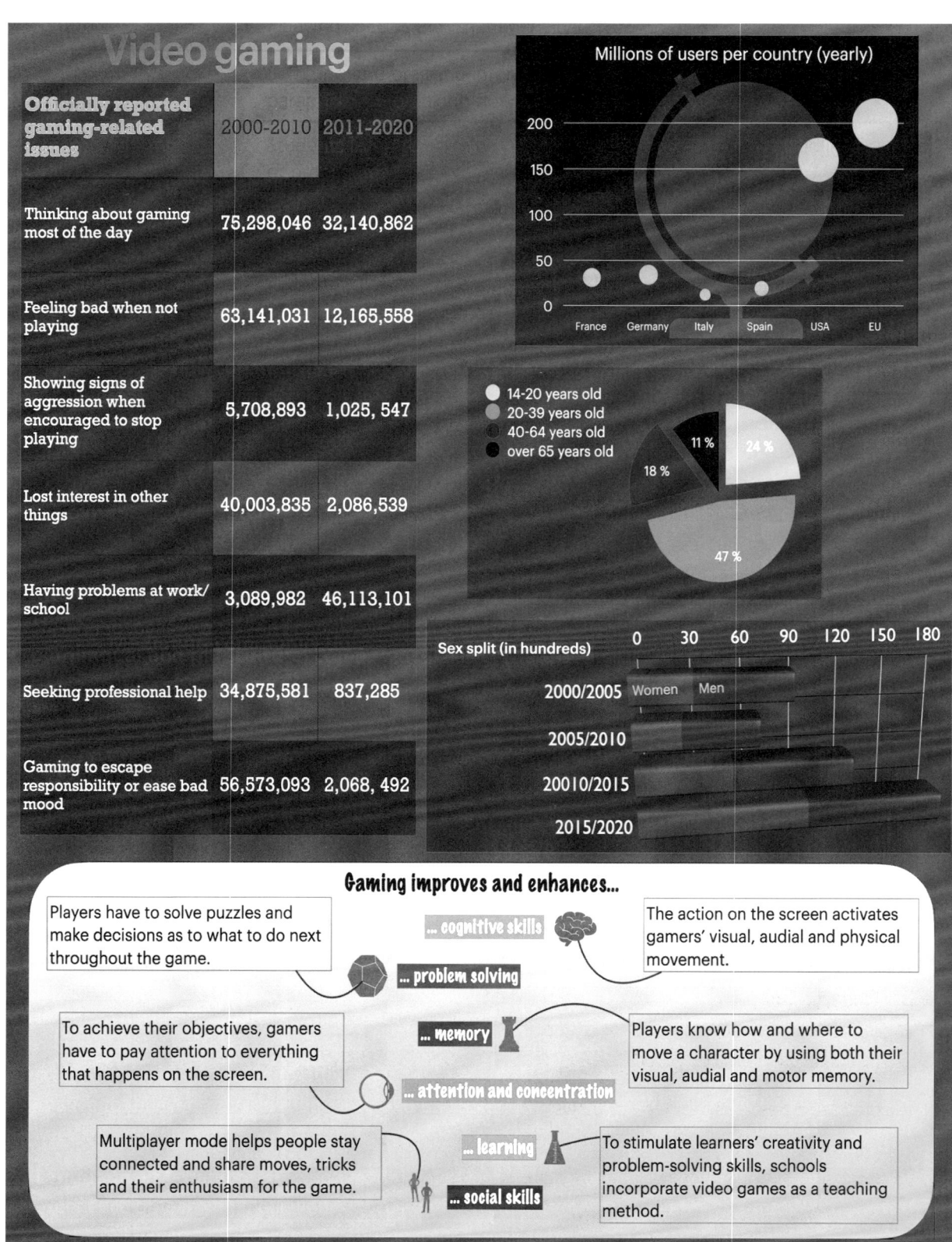

2.2a Gaming galore – the worksheet (Page 2/2)

Activity 2

Read the essay question below. Then, select the information from the infographic that you think you will need to answer the essay question.

> **ESSAY WANTED**
>
> A popular education magazine has asked its readers to write an essay answering the following question:
>
> *Some people believe that video games can be powerful educational tools. Others, on the other hand, just see them as toxic fun. In your opinion, do the drawbacks of playing video games outweigh the benefits?*
>
> Select appropriate information from the infographic to include in your essay.
>
> Write between 150 and 200 words.

Activity 3

To help you plan your essay, discuss the questions below with a partner.

Focus on target reader
- Who's likely to read your essay?
- What do you think they will know about the topic?
- What information about the topic do you think might be new or interesting to them?

Information from infographic
- What key information are you going to use to support your opinion to answer the essay question?
- What information are you going to do more research on before writing your essay?

Writing
- How many paragraphs are you going to write?
- What are you going to write in each of them?

Style and language
- Does your essay need to be formal or informal?
- What keywords from the infographic do you think you will have to use in your essay? And what other topic vocabulary do you think you will need to use?
- Language to compare and contrast information (e.g. comparatives and superlatives, linking words like however and nonetheless, etc.) is quite common in essays. What other type of language do you think you will need to use in your essay?

2.2b Write for me, please

 About the activity

Mediation task type	Explaining data
Mediation strategies	Selecting and omitting information, summarising, explaining
Summary of the activity	Students use visual, numerical and textual data to write an email to the customer service of an online shop for a friend with a limited proficiency of English.

Rationale

We are often called upon to help someone with a lower proficiency of a language we speak. This task gives students the opportunity to develop valuable mediation strategies for this common situation.

 How to run the activity

Levels	A2–B1	Learners	Teens/Adults	Time	45 minutes

Preparation	Make a copy of the worksheet below for each of your students.
Procedure	1. Lead into the topic by eliciting any bad experiences your students have had shopping online, e.g. late delivery, wrong orders, poor customer service. 2. Hand out **Worksheet** and organise class into pairs. Ask students to read the instructions and check their understanding. 3. Explain task: in pairs, students use the instructions and the visual information in the worksheet to write an email to the shop for their friend, Goran. In the email, they have to describe the situation and ask the shop to address the problem. 4. In pairs, students look at the information and write the email to the shop for Goran. 5. Ask students to stick their emails on the walls around the classroom. Invite students to read other pairs' emails and decide which email best explains/summarises the situation. 6. Collect the emails and prepare to give feedback.

Language	– Lexis related to online shopping: *cart, delivery, purchase, transfer*
	– Email language/phrases: *I am writing to let you know that…, I am looking forward to hearing from you,* etc.
	– Polite forms: *I would like to know…, Could you please let me know what/when…*
	– Functional language to
	  • explain: *This means that…, What happened/The problem is that…,* etc.
	  • contrast: *I've already paid for the product. However…, Although I can see the products in BUY AGAIN, they don't appear in…,* etc.

2.2b Write for me, please

▼▲ Differentiation	Challenge more confident students or fast finishers by asking them to roleplay what might happen next. A possible situation could be, for example, that the shop doesn't respond and so Goran's friend decides to call the shop manager or owner. In this case, your students could script and/or act out the phone call with the shop manager or owner.
Variation and extension	This task could be made cross-linguistic by giving students information in their own L1. To find/create the materials: - "Products ordered" section: find an online shop from your students' country/with information in your students' language and take screenshots of three to five products - "Bank payment details" and "Your orders" sections: write these yourself in a document. In case you aren't proficient in your students' language, ask the students themselves or a colleague to help you.
Feedback	This should focus on how well the students have understood Goran's situation, interpreted the data available and then explained the problem in their emails to the shop. The mediation strategies that students are brought to use in this task are summarising and explaining visual data, but other strategies you could focus on are - Adapting the language: have the students used an appropriate register (i.e. informal/neutral)? - Amplifying a dense text: have the students included helpful information (background information, details, explanatory comments, etc.)?
Adaptation for the virtual classroom	- For stage 4, ask students to type their email in a shared online document. - For stage 5, ask pairs to share their documents with all the class (and you) so that everyone can read them.

2.2b Write for me, please – the worksheet (Page 1/2)

Instructions

> **The situation**
>
> You live in the UK. Your friend Goran says he ordered some products from an online shop two weeks ago. He tells you that
> - he has already paid for the products
> - he hasn't received any email saying that the products have been sent
> - the information on the website of the online shop is not correct.
>
> Goran doesn't speak English well, so he shows you the information on his phone (below) and asks you to write an email to the shop for him.
>
> In the email, describe the situation using the information Goran has showed you, and ask the shop to explain what happened with the order.

Information

1. Products ordered

BUY NOW!
Online shop for mountain experts only

POTUR Trekking boots
£44.05
Waterproof suede
Vibram SPE midsole for maximum rebound, comfort and support.
Delivery time: UK – 3/4 days; EU – 10/15 days
Size UK8/EU43

VÄRMARE Thermal socks
£12.39
78% soft, breathable, high-quality cotton fibre
Delivery time: UK – 2/3 days; EU – 8/13 days
Size UK8-10/EU43/45

BRADSNOW Ski jacket
£66.50
Ergonomically designed
Waterproof & windproof
Delivery time: UK – 3/4 days; EU – 10/15 days
Size XL

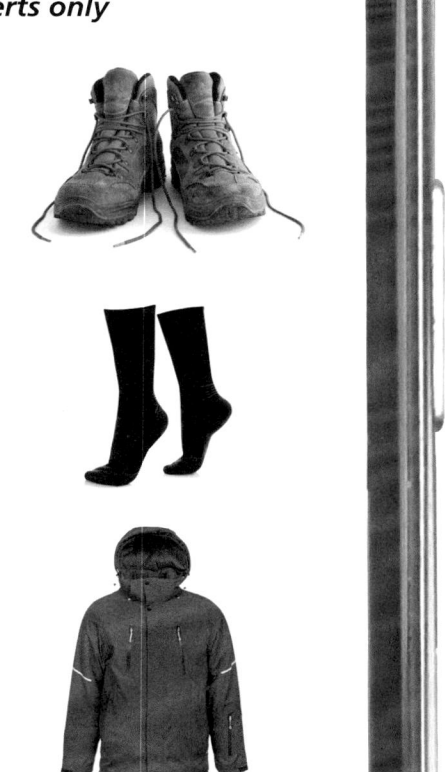

2.2b Write for me, please – the worksheet (Page 2/2)

2. "Your orders" section

Orders in progress

– You haven't made any orders yet. Start buying now!

Buy again

– EVENTOUR trekking boots – £44.05
– VÄRMARE thermal socks – £12.39
– BRADSNOW Ski jackets – £66.50

3. Bank payment details

Date	Description	Amount	Balance
9/6/2021	Payment BUYNOW ONLINESHOP	£122.94	£672.00

2.2c Elections

💡 About the activity

Mediation task type	Explaining data and processing text
Mediation strategies	Selecting and omitting information, transforming visual data into verbal text, expanding and/or summarising
Summary of the activity	Students identify relevant information in two source texts – an infographic about the US election process, and a video about the US electoral college voting system – and incorporate this into a critical essay (target text) for a university project.

Rationale

Extracting information from visual data and combining it with previous knowledge to write a critical text is a competence that is required by all types of students. Although the very first letter in the PARSNIP acronym, the topic of the task also lends itself to sociocultural discussion: by learning and being stimulated to give an opinion on a different political system, students have the opportunity to critically think about their own, an opportunity that opens that process of sociocultural awareness and that places them in a better position to engage in pluricultural discussion. <u>Before using this task, however, make sure it complies with your school's policies.</u>

▶ How to run the activity

Levels	B2–C1	Learners	Teens/Adults	Time	90 minutes (two 45-minute lessons)

Preparation	- Make a copy of **Essay instructions** for each of your students. - Print a copy of **Infographic Poster: How to Become President of the United States** for each of your students. - YouTube video: **Does your vote count? The Electoral College explained** - If you think that your students need to revise how to write a critical essay, do it immediately after stage 2 in Lesson 1 the procedure below.

2.2c Elections

Procedure	**Lesson 1** 1. Lead into the topic, for example, by eliciting what students know about the US presidential elections. 2. Explain task: over two lessons, students work in pairs to prepare and write an essay for their (e.g. social science/anthropology) project. In their essays, they have to include relevant information identified in and selected from two source texts – i.e. the infographic about the presidential elections process and the TED talks video on how the US electoral college voting system works – and combine this with what they already know about the topic. Hand out Essay instructions and allow time for students to understand the task. Check understanding before passing on to the next stage. 3. Organise class into pairs and hand out copies of the infographic. Together, students identify and agree on the key/relevant points for their essay. 4. Show TED talks video and ask students to take notes. Once the video is finished, ask students to compare with their partners and agree on the most important points (play the video as many times as necessary). 5. Pairs plan their essay deciding how to combine the information identified in both source texts in stages 3 and 4. 6. Once pairs have planned their essays, run conferencing activity in which, in a plenary, students can brainstorm ideas and help each other think of how to tackle the essay: they could compare their plans, say what they might talk about when covering the most important key points to include, and the reasons why they might do so. If students want to incorporate one or some of the points or solutions suggested by the other pairs, allow time for them to discuss it with their partners and make adjustments to their own plan as necessary. **Lesson 2** 7. Ask pairs to use the infographic and their notes from the previous class to write their essay. Monitor and assist as necessary. 8. Hand out the Peer-feedback sheet and explain the next stage: students read the other pairs' essays and give each other constructive feedback by answering the questions on the Peer-feedback sheet/assess them using the checklist. 9. Pairs swap essays: they read them and answer the questions in the Peer-feedback sheet/assess them using the checklist. 10. Pairs give each other constructive feedback. 11. Pairs make changes to their first draft and hand in their final draft. 12. Give feedback on the task.

2.2c Elections

Language	- Lexis: *caucuses, convention, primaries, running mate*
	- Sequencers: *Firstly, the members of the party meet in a caucus, Once ballots are collected…*
	- Passives: *If the candidate is found not eligible, then he or she can…, A candidate might receive more votes than their opponent, but…*
	- Functional language to
	  • generalise: *Generally, …/As a general rule, …*
	  • contrast information: *However, each candidate can receive roughly the same percentage of votes and…, Although there are fifty states in the USA, only few are considered…*
	  • exemplify: *such as, for instance, e.g.*

▼▲ Differentiation	- Some students might benefit from looking at an outline of a plan for a critical essay – provide them with summary of the content that should be included in each paragraph, or even a general list of tips, such as *include a title that summarises the topic or introduce by explaining what the essay is about and make your opinion clear from the start*, etc. - Provide extra language for less-confident/lower-level students (e.g. how to introduce, how to conclude, how to describe, explain, etc.)
Variation and extension	Cross-linguistic mediation (only for monolingual groups): ask your students to mediate information about the election system in their own country using visual, written or spoken texts in their own language. If you're proficient in your students' language, find the source materials yourself. Otherwise, ask your students or a colleague to help you.

Feedback	This should focus on
	- how well the question for the essay has been answered.
	- how accurately the data from the source texts have been interpreted and incorporated into the target text;
	- how this has been used to support the student/writer's view in the essay.
	
	Some other areas and questions you could focus on are:
	
	1. Genre:
	  • *Does the essay answer the question? Is the content relevant for the target reader?*
	  • *Does the text respect the typical genre features of an essay* (layout, organisation, style, language, etc.)?
	
	2. Mediation strategies:
	  • *Has the data been critically selected and omitted?*
	  • *How has it been used (i.e. explained, expanded on, summarised, etc.) in the essay?*

Adaptation for the virtual classroom	- Share the handout. - You can run stages 3 to 5, 7, 9, 10 and 11 using breakout rooms, whereas you need to do stages 1, 2, 6, 8 and 12 in the main room.

2.2c Elections – Essay instructions

1.

> **ESSAY WANTED**
>
> *Is the US presidential election system fair?*
>
> Your school has been working on a project together with a foreign partner school. The project is called "Fair political elections in the world". In your class, you have discussed the US presidential elections and now your teacher has asked you to do further research and write a critical essay on the topic. The best essay will be published in the magazine of your foreign partner school.
>
> Write between (e.g. 150–200) words.

2. Link to infographic:
   https://www.usa.gov/election

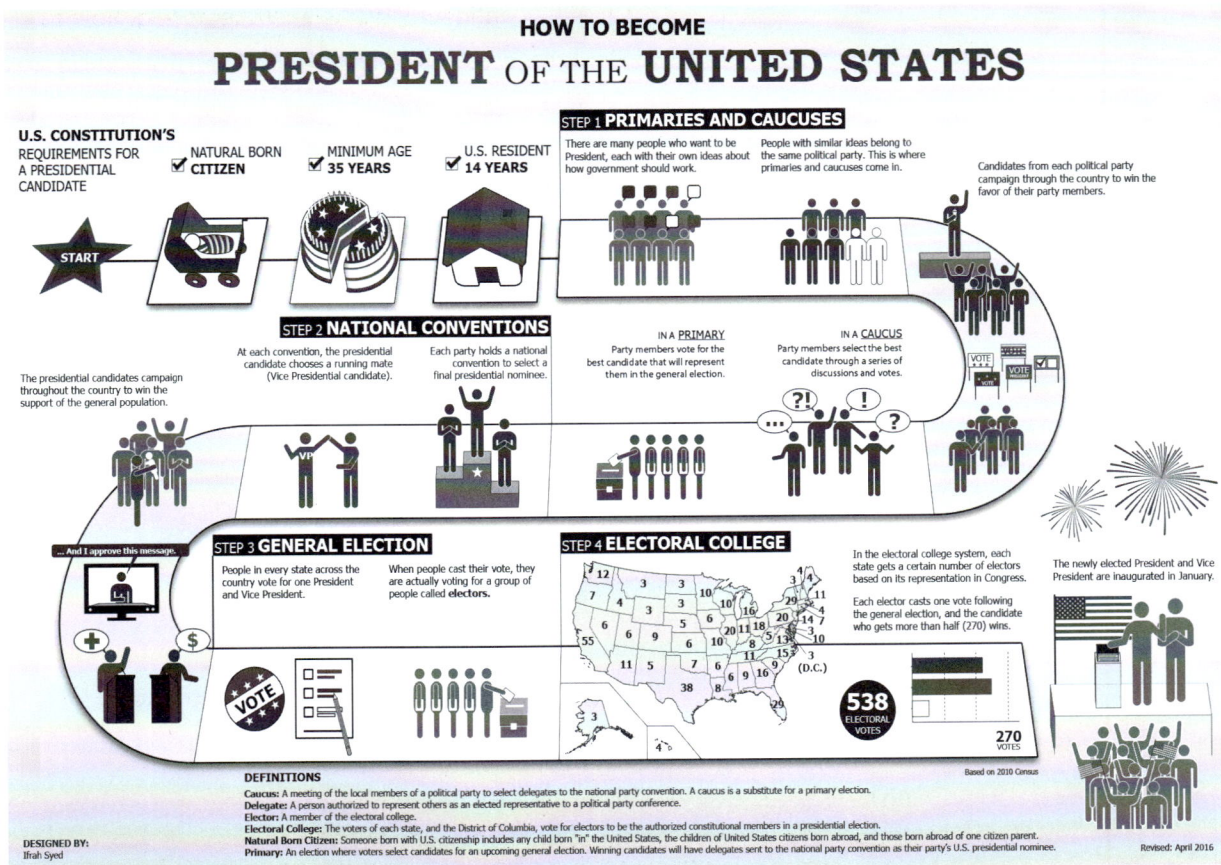

3. Link to video:
   https://www.ted.com/talks/christina_greer_does_your_vote_count_the_electoral_college_explained?language=en

2.2c Elections – Peer-feedback sheet

ESSAY

1. Content
   - Does the essay answer the question?
   - Are there any important points that have been left out? Why?

   ....
   ....
   ....
   ....

2. Communicative achievement
   - Is the information clear?
   - Are there any parts that need further explaining, exemplifying? Which ones? Why?

   ....
   ....
   ....
   ....

3. Mediation strategies
   - Find examples of information that was transferred from the infographic and video to the essay. Which information was
     - paraphrased?
     - explained?
     - expanded on?
     - left as it was in the original text?

   ....
   ....
   ....
   ....

4. What I particularly liked – write maximum three.

   ....
   ....
   ....

5. What can be improved – write maximum three.

   ....
   ....
   ....

_____ 2.2d Metanotes

2.2d Metanotes

 About the activity

Mediation task type	Note-taking and processing text
Mediation strategies	Summarising, paraphrasing, breaking down complicated information
Summary of the activity	Students listen to part of a seminar and take notes of the key points and ideas. Then, they put their notes together and write the missing paragraphs of an incomplete article about the same topic.

Rationale

In this task, students will expand on their knowledge of and techniques for note-taking, and to use notes productively

 How to run the activity

Levels	B2–C1	**Learners**	Teens/Adults	**Time**	60 minutes

Preparation	− Make a copy of the introduction of the article for each of your students. − As this is a jigsaw listening activity, different students will be listening to a different recording. For this reason: • prepare to share Recording 1, 2 and 3 with your students (DELTA Augmented), and • make sure your students can use headphones or, if this isn't possible, that they can find a quiet spot in the school where they can listen to the recording (e.g. corridor, library, other empty rooms).
Procedure	1. Lead in by discussing the topic of note-taking in open class. For example, you could ask students when and how they take notes, how they use their notes once they've taken them, etc. 2. Hand out the introduction of the article and explain that the article is incomplete. Ask students to read the introduction and identify the topic of the article (note-taking). 3. Divide the class into groups of three and explain task: students listen to different parts of a seminar and take notes on key points and ideas. Assign roles and recordings: • Students A listen to Recording 1: *Linear methods 1 and 2* • Students B listen to Recording 2: *Non-linear method 1* • Students C listen to Recording 3: *Non-linear method 2* **Note:** If your students can use headphones, they don't need to leave the classroom, but if they don't, help them find a quiet spot outside the classroom (corridor, library, etc.) where they can listen to the recording they've been assigned.

2.2d Metanotes

Procedure	4. Students listen to the recording they've been assigned and summarise the content in the form of notes. 5. Students regroup. Using their notes, they relay the information they've just learnt from the recording to their partners. 6. Working in the same groups, students complete the article adding the missing sections. First, each student writes a draft of his/her own section. Then, together with their partners, they edit the article to include the four missing sections and make appropriate changes to match the style and language of the introduction. **Notes:** 1. It might be a good idea to set a time limit for students to complete their own section of the article. 2. For the conclusion of the article (i.e. "Finally, I'll briefly tell you which of the four methods I've decided to try myself in my next class, conference or meeting."), ask students to agree on which of the four methods from the recordings they want to talk about and try. Another option could be simply to ask them to each write their own version of the conclusion individually. 7. Collect articles and prepare to give feedback.

Language	- Lexis to
	  • talk about note-taking: *categorise, jot down, (make a) mental note of (something), sub-topic*
	  • describe diagrams and non-linear notes in general: *charting, concept mapping, hierarchical order, represent*
	- Informal expressions to organise discourse: *another method that is worth mentioning is, what's more, though, to sum/wrap up*
	- Functional language to
	  • explain: *Let's say that we are/have…, It's like when we/you…*
	  • paraphrase: *In other words, put another way*
	  • summarise: *Basically…, In short…*

Differentiation	- Some students might find their recording challenging. In this case, allow them to continue listening to their recording on their smartphones, school's computers or tablets as many times as necessary. You could also make the audio scripts available. - Some students might not finish their article by the end of the lesson. Allow them to hand in their article in the next class or ask them to send it to you by email, etc. - Stronger students or fast finishers can spend more time focussing on the different features of the genre. Encourage them to suggest more edits for style, language, etc. when working with their partners in stage 7.

2.2d Metanotes

Variation and extension	Instead of an article, students can be asked to complete a blog post or prepare a script and record a vlog post. In this case, remember to make appropriate changes to the **Introduction to the article** in the Materials section below and turn it into "Introduction to the blog" or "vlog".
Feedback	This should focus on how well the students have been able to - select and summarise the main points and ideas from the recordings into their notes - relay the information to their partners using their notes - combine with the main points from each recording in the article
Adaptation for the virtual classroom	- Share the digital version of the worksheet with your students. **Introduction to the article**. - Send students into individual breakout rooms for stage 4. This will allow you to monitor and assist them better.

2.2d Metanotes – Introduction of the article

TO TAKE OR NOT TO TAKE NOTES? AND HOW?

Who took the first note ever? Was it the Neanderthals? The Mesopotamians? The Egyptians? No one really knows, unfortunately. But one thing we do seem to know: the ancient Greeks were the first ones on record to give it a name. "Hypopnema" they called it, which, in English, often gets translated as "reminder", "note" or even "draft".

But it's not the history of note-taking that I'll be lecturing you on, here. First, I'll give you two examples of what are called "linear" methods of taking notes. Then, I'll talk about two other methods that are instead called "non-linear". Finally, I'll briefly tell you which of these four methods I've decided to try and use myself in my next class, conference or meeting.

- Missing section 1 (Linear methods 1 and 2)

- Missing section 2 (Non-linear method 1)

- Missing section 3 (Non-linear method 2)

- Missing section 4 (Conclusion)

2.2d Metanotes – the audioscripts

Recording 1 – Linear methods 1 and 2

Note-taking is an important skill for students and professionals alike.

In some contexts, such as university lectures or business meetings, the main purpose of taking notes may be to implant the material in our own mind or even pass on the information to someone else who could not attend the lecture or meeting.

As taking notes is a mental process, each of us will find a method more useful than others, but all of these methods do fall into just two main types, namely "linear" and "non-linear" methods.

We take "linear notes" when we write down pieces of information in the same order as we read or hear them. In this category, there are two main methods that are popular among students and professionals alike: "Outlining" and "Sentence method".

"Outlining" is when we write down our notes in a logical and structured way. If I use this method, it means that I would first write down the main topic and then list down the different sub-topics, categorising them, for example, as sub-topic A, B, C, or 1, 2, 3 and so on. For each of these sub-topics, then, I might need to write down further sub-sections, either in the form of a list or separating them with dashes, slashes and so on.

"Sentence writing", on the other hand, is when we write down the topics we read or hear in full sentences, short or long that they might be. Although this seems like a difficult task, there are many people I personally know that are able to write full sentences that actually make sense if it's someone else that reads them at the end of a lecture or meeting. Anyway, linear methods seem to work quite well with pretty much all types of information, but there are people working in certain fields such as science, law or economics, for instance, who actually prefer non-linear methods.

(315 words – approx. 3 minutes)

Recording 3 – Non-linear method 2

Using non-linear notes doesn't mean writing our notes in a way that is not logical or structured. Some techniques might sure look a bit messy on the page if read by someone else who did not write the notes in the first place.

Shorthand notes, for example, would look more like an impossible code to decipher to someone who doesn't know how to use this method, whereas other more common non-linear systems, such as concept mapping or charting, look pretty professional and neat, and therefore useful to memorise and learn the information gathered.

Through mapping and charting we summarise information in boxes, circles and other forms and shapes, and we create a hierarchical order for them, for example by adding and linking the different sub-topics we read or hear to the main topic or topics, categorising them in tidy, smaller boxes or circles and so on, and expanding on the main topic.

2.2d Metanotes – the audioscripts

This is what some of my colleagues and I do to prepare for a seminar or presentation, for example, or even to plan a book or an article.

But say that we are marketing professionals designing a campaign for a new product and we have a problem to face and solve. In this case, we might prefer using an Ishikawa diagram, most commonly known as a "fishbone" diagram. To organise information using this type of noting system, we would first draw a horizontal line, that is, the fish's spine. Then, we'd write the problem on the right end of the spine – say, "pollution". The problem would represent the fish's head. Above and below the fish's spine, we would then write the factors contributing to or the causes we identify for the problem, say, "fossil fuels", "waste", "mining", for example, and we'd place them above and below the spine. These factors would represent the different fish's bones. Some will be bigger and therefore more important, while others will be smaller or less important.

(323 words – approx. 3 minutes)

Recording 3 – Non-linear method 2

"Cornell notes" is a non-linear method developed by Walter Pauk in the 1940s and published in his book, How to study in college, in 1974.

Although more than 50 years have passed since the publication of his book, Pauk's method seems to be still very popular among American college and university students.

What we do with Cornell notes is quite simple: we divide the page of our notebook into three sections: two columns for our notes – that is, one column on the left of the page and one on the right – and then a rectangular box at the bottom of the page.

In the left column, we would write the topics or keywords that we're doing research on – if we're working on a written assignment or oral presentation from our home or office, for example – or that you're listening for when attending a lecture or conference. The right column, which should be at least twice the size of the left column, is for us to fill in with notes corresponding to each of the topics or keywords that we placed in the left column. In the box that we've left at the bottom of the page, on the other hand, we can write a summary of the most important concepts from the notes in an even more condensed way, or we can jot down our own reflections on the material learnt so that it can also serve us as a learning journal any time we want to go back and review that lesson and check what we have learnt or need to study more.

I'm a fan of Cornell notes myself, but one suggestion that I always give my students is to find their own layout themselves, be it on their notebooks, on their laptop or tablet. Instead of two columns and a box, for example, they can have three columns and a different order in which they appear on the page.

(324 words – approx. 3 minutes)

2.3a A fairy tale for children

 About the activity

Mediation task type	Processing text
Mediation strategies	Selecting and omitting information, paraphrasing, linking to previous knowledge, combining, adapting language
Summary of the activity	Students adapt a narrative into a children's fairy tale. They will do this by keeping, changing, eliminating as well as adding elements in their new narrative so as to make it (more) suitable to the abilities and level of maturity of the new target audience.
Materials	• The tips sheet • A video

Rationale

The objective of adapting a text is to make its content more appropriate and relevant to a new audience. To do this successfully, besides summarising or expanding, explaining and paraphrasing, we might also need to reshape the very concepts and ideas contained in the source text, or even its genre and register. And adapting information for younger audiences is indeed a good opportunity for students to practise these key mediation strategies.

 How to run the activity

Levels	B2–C1	Learners	Teens/Adults	Time	45–60 minutes

Preparation	– Find an appropriate short film whose target audience is 7+ or older, such as One Rat Short (2006), Worlds Apart (2011) or One Small Step (2018). Make sure you note down the target audience age group for later. Suggested length of the film: 5–10 minutes. – Print a copy of **the tips sheet** for each student.
Procedure	1. Tell students they are going to watch a short film. When they finish, they have to answer these questions: • *What is the short film about?* • *What age do you think it is intended for? Why?* 2. Students watch the short film and answer questions. 3. Ask students to compare their answers with a partner. Then, tell them what age range the short film is intended for.

2.3a A fairy tale for children

Procedure	4. Organise class into pairs and explain the task: students have to adapt the short film into a written fairy tale for pre-school children (3–5 years old). To do this, they will have to decide on which elements from the film they would like to keep, eliminate, change or add in their fairy tale (e.g. the sequence of the main events, the personality of a character, their names, the objects they use, etc.). 5. Hand out **the tips sheet**. Allow time for students to read through the tips and ask questions to check their understanding. 6. Students watch the short film for the second time. Using the information in **the tips sheet** as reference, they take notes on what they would like to keep, eliminate, change or add in their fairy tale. 7. Students compare their notes with their partners. Together, they agree on what to keep, eliminate, change or add in their fairy tale and write it. 8. Once pairs have finished writing their fairy tales, help them stick these up on the walls around the classroom. Then, ask them to read each other's fairy tales and look for similarities and differences between these and their own tales (e.g. the new elements included, the ones that have been altered or left out, etc). 9. In open class, have your students share their opinion about the fairy tales they've read and encourage them to tell each other how and why they came up with a certain idea, solution, character, etc. 10. Give feedback on the task.

Language	- Common words, phrases and expressions found in fairy tales: *Once (upon a time)…, And they (all) lived happily ever after, heroine/villain, cast a spell*
	- Linking devices such as conjunctions and discourse markers: *afterwards, although, as soon as, so*
	- Narrative tenses: *It was snowing that night…, She tiptoed back into the living room, left the key where she had found it and ran away.*
	- (For stage 4). Functional language to
	  • suggest: *What if we changed/added/scrapped…?*
	  • explain: *This might help the children understand…, in other words*
	  • summarise points made during the conversation: *As we all agreed…, So far, we have…*

▼▲ Differentiation	Before stage 3, provide less confident, lower-level or younger students with suggestions about what to focus on when adapting the original narrative to the age-group specified (e.g. characters, elements to include, style, etc.). To make sure they have this information available during the task, give them a written list of tips like the one in **the tips sheet**.

2.3a A fairy tale for children

Variation and extension	- Source text
	  • Instead of using videos, you can use written texts like short stories and poems, as well as spoken texts like anecdotes or even jokes.
	  • Students could use source materials in their own L1 (e.g. a folk tale that contains elements not suitable for children, a national film that everyone has seen or knows about, a joke, etc.).
	- Target text
	  • Instead of a tale, students could draw and write a picture book or roleplay a situation in which the "adults" tell their story, while the "children" listen and participate with questions and comments.
	  • Instead of a fairy tale, older/higher-level students can be encouraged to decide the genre of the target text themselves. Nonfiction and technical literature lends particularly well to this type of variation (e.g. writing a children's illustrated encyclopaedia entry to adapt one found in a regular encyclopaedia).
	- This activity could also easily be adapted for the higher-primary and lower-secondary CLIL classrooms. The topic lends itself to both age groups and provides a good opportunity to develop critical thinking (e.g. *What can children understand from the original story?, How can I make them "see" the main point/s in the original story? Which elements should I keep or change to do this?*) as well as creativity (changing, altering characters, making up new locations, events with the same characters, etc.). Also note that, depending on your students' age group, you should adapt the tips and examples in **the tips sheet**.

Feedback	This should focus on how well the students have combined their ideas to create their fairy tale, as well as how well they have adapted the main message of the original text in the new narrative. Some questions that teachers could answer while monitoring may be: - *How have students participated as groups?* - *How has each student contributed to group work?* - *Does the tale contain everyone's ideas?* - *Has the main message of the original text been respected?* - *Which elements were kept/removed/changed/added? Why?* - *Is the new text appropriate for the target audience? Why?*
Adaptation for the virtual classroom	While in their breakout rooms in stages 4 and 5, students could simultaneously - write their fairy tale by sharing and working on the same document, or - prepare to tell their fairy tale by sharing and working on the same slides. Once back in the main room, they will all be able to - share their written tales with the teacher and other students through the chat box, or - share their screens to tell their fairy tale and show their slides or drawings.

2.3a A fairy tale for children – the tips sheet

Work in pairs. Use the tips in the table below to adapt the short film into a fairy tale.

───────── KEEP ─────────
- what you think 3–5-year-old children CAN understand (e.g. *a hungry wolf*)
- the main message, moral or desired effect intended for the original target audience (e.g. *following someone's advice*)

───────── ELIMINATE ─────────
- what children CAN'T understand (e.g. *why people act so differently depending on the circumstances*)
- inappropriate messages, concepts or references

───────── CHANGE ─────────
- violence or other negative elements into more acceptable alternatives (e.g. *a fight that doesn't happen because a better and more peaceful solution is found*)
- frightening scenes/situations into amusing (e.g. *make a scary character look silly instead*)
- complex actions, characters, concepts, objects into ideas that are more easily understood by children (e.g. *instead of a "moody" character, choose one that is either evil or good and changes attitude only once at some point in the story*)
- complex situations into more linear or easy to understand (e.g. *if the original story starts from the end, follow a chronological order in your fairy tale instead*)

───────── ADD ─────────
- an element of magic (e.g. *a magic wand, a spell, a potion*)
- a hero/heroine (e.g. *a superhero or superheroine with superpowers*)
- a villain (e.g. *a wicked witch, an evil wizard, an angry troll*)
- a happy (and, if possible, constructive) ending (e.g. *"And they all lived happily ever after.", "And from that day on, she never had porridge for breakfast."*)

2.3b Cultural (con)version

 About the activity

Mediation task type	Processing text
Mediation strategies	Selecting and omitting information, summarising, paraphrasing, combining, explaining sociocultural elements
Summary of the activity	Students watch a short animated film and then adapt it by replacing elements from the original story with ones from their own culture.

Rationale

This task gives students the opportunity to further develop their awareness of cultural references in creative texts and encourages them to reflect on possible sociolinguistic and sociocultural differences between the culture represented in the text and their own.

How to run the activity

Levels	B1–B2	Learners	Teens/Adults	Time	45–60 minutes

Preparation	– Find a short animated film whose setting and characters are different from your students' country and culture. Decide whether to show the video in open class or email/airdrop the link to your students individually. – Make a copy of the **Adapt it!** grid for each of your students. **Note:** To run the task in one lesson, make sure the video isn't too long.
Procedure	1. Lead into the activity by putting a number of keywords from the short film on the board. In pairs or small groups, students predict what the short will be about. 2. Play video. Students watch the short and check their predictions from stage 1. 3. Give a copy of the **Adapt it!** grid to each of your students and explain task: in pairs, students have to create a "cultural conversion" of the original short film. They discuss which elements from the original story (e.g. setting, characters, events, etc.) they could replace using elements from their own culture. Encourage them to write their notes in the grid. **Note**: Use the examples in the second column in the **Adapt it!** grid. Also, explain to students that there is no limit as to which cultural elements they could use: these can be places and public personalities in their country, but also food and simple daily routines that are typical of their culture. 4. Pairs use the **Adapt it!** grid to create their "cultural conversion" of the short and prepare to tell it in open class.

2.3b Cultural (con)version

Procedure	5. Pairs tell their stories in open class. While listening, students take notes and prepare questions for the storytellers. 6. Storytellers answer questions and explain the reasons behind their changes, replacements, etc. 7. Give feedback on the task.

Language	- Common words and phrases for short narratives: *Once…, …ever again.*
	- Narrative tenses: *She walked some more and…, She was looking out of the window when…,*
	- Sequencers: *before, first, then, in the end*
	- Time adverbs and adverbials: *When the "carabiniere" turned the lights on…, After that, the politician ran outside and…*
	- (For stage 8). Functional language to
	  • express cause and result: *We chose the scooter because…, It's something that we/Italians normally do so…*
	  • contrast: *Instead of a girl, we decided to…, It's different, actually…*

▼▲ Differentiation	Some students might struggle with finding good equivalents or substitutes in their own culture: include stages or activities in which students share their ideas with the rest of the class and inspire each other (conferencing).
Variation and extension	- To give the task a more entertaining and funny twist, ask your students to create a parody of the original story instead. They could include elements from popular films and books as well as their own personal experiences. - For multilingual groups, each of your students can create their own "cultural version" of the source text. Even in this case, though, do allow them to work in pairs to discuss and explain what they plan to change in their own version.
Feedback	This should focus on how well the students have integrated the new cultural elements in the original story. Some questions that you might want to ask yourself while monitoring could be: - Can the students retell the story using elements from their own culture? - Is the text coherent? Does it stand on its own? - What new elements work particularly well? - Which new elements do not work particularly well?
Adaptation for the virtual classroom	Set up a class journal folder and share it with your students. Encourage them to write their reflections on sociocultural topics. For example, they could write about what new cultural things they have learnt, and whether they might have changed their mind with respect to certain topics throughout the course.

2.3b Cultural (con)version – Adapt it!

ELEMENTS IN THE ORGINAL STORY	EXAMPLE VERSION: *My Italian Red Riding Hood*	YOUR VERSION
Setting	<ul><li>replace woods with ROME'S TRAFFIC FILLED STREETS</li><li>replace grandma's house with MY GRANDMA'S OLD FIAT</li></ul>	
Characters	<ul><li>replace wolf with a BAD POLITICIAN</li><li>replace hunter with CARABINIERE</li></ul>	
Beginning	<ul><li>replace basket to grandma with PANETTONE</li></ul>	
End	<ul><li>hunter doesn't kill the wolf, but the CARABINIERE ARRESTS THE BAD POLITICIAN</li></ul>	
Other	<ul><li>Red Riding Hood doesn't walk in the woods but RIDES HER SCOOTER WITH HER RED HELMET ON</li></ul>	

2.3c Tips for new parents

About the activity

Mediation task type	Processing text
Mediation strategies	Selecting and omitting information, summarising, paraphrasing
Summary of the activity	Students deliver a short monologue in which they pass on key points and ideas from an article.

Rationale

In our daily lives, we often summarise the contents of a text for another person who has not had the time or opportunity to read, watch or listen to it. In the act of closing this type of "information gap," we use a variety of mediation strategies that students can develop in class.

How to run the activity

Levels	B2–C1	Learners	Adults	Time	30 minutes

Preparation	Make enough copies of worksheets A and B so that every student in the class has either A or B. Cut the peer-feedback worksheet along the dotted line.
Procedure	1. Lead into the topic by organising the class into pairs and asking students to make a list of challenges to becoming a new parent. 2. Hand out worksheet A to half the pairs and worksheet B to the other half. 3. Give them time to read the rubric and then ask a few questions to check their understanding of this task, e.g. *How long is your monologue?* 4. Students read the text individually. Then organise the class into AA and BB pairs. With partner, who has also read the same text, they discuss what information they think would be important to include in their monologues. Together they fill out the mind map. Note that mind maps are a very good strategy for this type of spoken mediation task. They help students organise their monologues and students are less likely to run out of things to say. 5. Regroup the students into AB pairs. Explain the task: students deliver their monologues while their partners assess them using the peer-feedback form. Remind them to time themselves and respect the time limit. 6. Pass out the appropriate peer-feedback form (A or B). 7. Students take turns doing their monologues, while partners listen and assess them.

2.3c Tips for new parents

Procedure	8. When both students have finished, they take turns giving each other feedback. Circulate and take notes on what the students did particularly well and where they could still improve. 9. Give feedback on the task.
Language	– Lexis related the topic of parenting: *calm, happy memories, create a strong relationship* – Functional language for: • Referring to the source text: *From what I've read…, in the article it says…, According to the article…* • Sequencing information: *First of all… Another interesting point is that… It's also true that…* • Making a recommendation: *If I were you, I would…, You really must make time to…, You should try to…*
▼▲ Differentiation	– Some students may find it uncomfortable to be assessed by peers, perceiving this as the "teacher's job." In this case, explain the value of peer feedback: while they assess their classmates, students will be improving their own ability to tackle spoken mediation tasks, as well as becoming more autonomous learners. An alternative would be to have students record themselves doing the monologue, and then assess themselves using the appropriate peer-feedback form. – For adult students who have children, you could ask for their opinion on the advice given in the texts.
Variation and extension	Students could have a second go at their monologues after receiving feedback from their classmates. If there is time, you could round off the lesson with a general discussion of the topic in small groups or open class. Possible questions for this stage could include: > • Being a new parent is very tiring. Which do you think would be easier for parents of young children to find the time and energy to do, singing or reading? > • What other activities are good to do with young children? > • What advice would you give to parents of young children related to nutrition? This intralinguistic mediation task could be transformed into a cross-linguistic one by replacing the English source texts with texts on the same topic in the students' L1, or by choosing two texts on a different topic and modifying the task instructions accordingly.

2.3c Tips for new parents

Feedback	This should focus on how well students: a. select the key points and ideas in the source text b. paraphrase these key points and incorporate them into their monologues, along with their own opinion c. deliver a well-organised monologue that is easy to follow and understand, as well as being in the appropriate register. If students include too much extra information, i.e. specific examples or supporting evidence rather than just key points, lead an open class discussion about why it would not be necessary to include this kind of information.
Adaptation for the virtual classroom	The pair work activities could be done in breakout rooms. However, you would have to assign the students to breakout rooms manually in order to create the AB pairs for the monologue stage, instead of allowing the video conferencing programme to create them automatically.

2.3c Tips for new parents – worksheet A

Student A

Your favourite podcast has asked its listeners to contribute to the show by sending a short voice message on the topic of "tips for parents of young children." Read the article and then deliver a short monologue (2–3 minutes) in which you:
- Summarise the main points and ideas
- Recommend that parents sing to their babies

Why every parent should sing to their babies (even if they are not good singers)

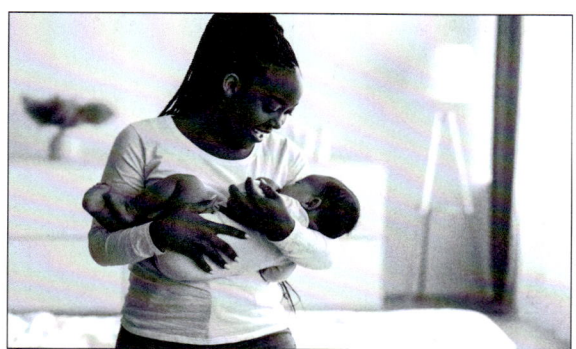

Singing to babies is natural. Parents all over the world seem to have an instinct to sing to their newborns—and small babies love it. Here are a few good reasons to sing to your baby.

It's a special bonding time.
Singing to babies helps create a strong bond between parents and their children. When singing to your baby, you smile and look into their eyes. This sends the message to babies that they are important, that their parents love them, that they are the centre of their parents' universe.

It helps with communication.
Singing is a particularly good way of communicating with your baby. With a song, you can tell your baby that they are safe and the world around them is gentle and calm. With another type of song, you can communicate that life is fun and happy.

It helps parents too!
Being a new parent is not always easy. Singing can help parents feel less stressed out and better able to deal with the frustrations of parenting. When parents sing to their children, they feel like more competent parents, which makes them feel happier and more satisfied.

It makes children more intelligent
When babies listen to their parents sing, they develop the skill of listening for long periods of time. They learn to concentrate. Not only that, babies also learn new language sounds and words, just like when they do when you read them a book. And singing the same song again and again is a great way of improving a baby's memory.

So, all you new parents out there, don't worry if you only know one song or if you can't sing well. Your baby will love your songs even better than those sung by a professional.

Before you deliver your monologue, use the mind map below to organise your ideas.

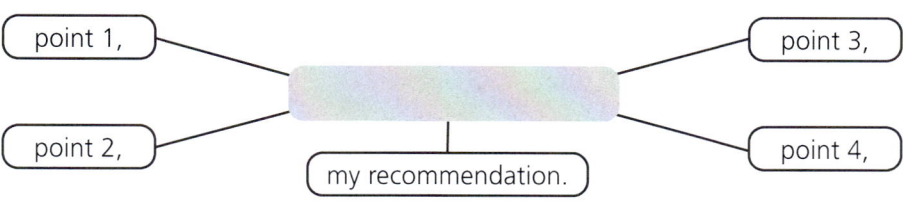

2.3c Tips for new parents – worksheet B

Student B

Your favourite podcast has asked its listeners to contribute to the show by sending a short voice message on the topic of "tips for parents of young children." Read the article and then deliver a short monologue (2–3 minutes) in which you:
- Summarise the main points and ideas
- Recommend that parents read to their children

The important benefits of reading to children

Reading is not only one of the most special activities you can engage in with your children, it is also arguably the most important. Why? Here are a few good reasons.

Language skills
To begin with, reading to children helps them learn their mother tongue. A recent study of the human brain found that reading with children activates parts of the brain associated with understanding language. While reading, children of course learn pronunciation, but also grammar. And they acquire vocabulary as well – lots and lots of it!

Imagination
But reading does not only improve children's language skills; it also helps them use their imaginations. As you read to a child, they visualize the events of the book in their minds. They have the opportunity to explore places, times and events outside of their daily life. It opens doors to new worlds. What is more, research shows that if you read to children, they are better at creating stories from their own imaginations.

Bonding time
Did you know that reading helps create a strong relationship between you and your child? If it is part of your daily routine, for example, before bed, you create a special time when your child can look forward to spending time with you. This "bonding time" helps children experience intimacy, the feeling of being close to someone who loves them.

Lifetime interest in reading
Children who read associate this activity with happy memories. Children who learn to enjoy independent reading will probably continue to read as adults, which will help them be more successful in school and at work. As the famous children's book writer Dr Seuss says, "The more you read, the more things you will know. The more that you learn, the more places you'll go."

Before you deliver your monologue, use the mind map below to organise your ideas.

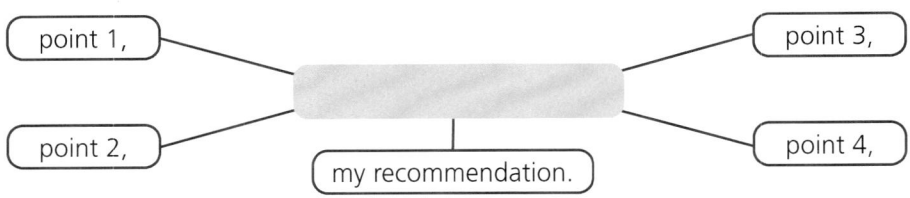

2.3c Tips for new parents – the peer-feedback forms

Student A peer-feedback form

1. Listen to your partner's monologue. Do they include the following main points and ideas?
   - Reading to children helps them learn their parents' language.
   - Reading helps children develop their imaginations.
   - Reading helps create a strong relationship between children and their parents.
   - Children who read will be more interested in reading when they grow up.

2. Does your partner include their own opinion?

3. Is the monologue well-organised?

4. Is it easy to understand and follow what your partner says?

Student B peer-feedback form

1. Listen to your partner's monologue. Do they include the following main points and ideas?
   - Singing helps create a strong relationship between babies and their parents.
   - With a song, you can communicate important emotions and messages.
   - When parents sing to babies, it makes them feel like good parents.
   - Singing makes babies smarter.

2. Does your partner include their own opinion?

3. Is the monologue well-organised?

4. Is it easy to understand and follow what your partner says?

2.3d Running dictogloss*

About the activity

Mediation task type	Processing text
Mediation strategies	Selecting and omitting information, summarising, paraphrasing, translating
Summary of the activity	One student relays in English the key points of a text in their L1 to another student who has not read it. With the help of their partner, the second student writes a short summary.

Rationale

This task puts a plurilingual, student-centred twist on the popular dictogloss activity. During the task, students develop valuable mediation strategies applicable to common real-life situations involving mediation of information from L1 to L2.

▶ How to run the activity

Levels	B2–C1	Learners	Teens/Adults	Time	30 minutes

Preparation	- Find an informational text in the student's L1, e.g. an article about deforestation in your students' country. - Locate the key points and paraphrase them yourself in English, in order to have a suggested answer key to check the students' work. - Make a copy of the text in the L1 for each pair and put them up on the classroom wall before the start of the lesson.
Procedure	1. Lead into the lesson by asking what the students already know about the topic of the text you've chosen and what they would like to learn about it. 2. Explain the activity and organise the students into pairs. 3. While students relay the information and write their summaries, go around the class and monitor, providing support when appropriate. 4. When the students have finished their summaries, put two pairs together to make a group of four. Together, the students share and compare, reflecting on the key points in the source text and how they chose to paraphrase these and incorporate them into their summaries.

* The idea for this activity came from the late Tim Goodier, one of the co-authors of the CEFRCV.

2.3d Running dictogloss

Procedure	5. In open class, elicit the key points and give feedback on the task. If students include too much extra information, i.e. specific examples or supporting evidence rather than just key points, lead a discussion about why this type of information would not normally be included in a summary. This is a good time to work with any lexical items or concepts from the students' L1 that they had a hard time translating into English. 6. At the end of the activity, collect the summaries in order to provide more detailed written feedback.
Language	– Lexis related to the topic of the text, e.g. *clear the land, construct new roads*, and *loss of biodiversity* (for a text about deforestation) – Functional language for: • Discussing translation: *I think in English you would say… I'm not quite sure how to say this in English, but…* • Summarising: *One of the main ideas is… In general, what the writer is trying to say is that…* • Referring to the source text: *In the text it says… So, according to what I read…*
▼▲ Differentiation	– To add a bit of extra scaffolding, you may want to consider pre-teaching a few difficult lexical items from the text. This could be done by having students match items in their L1 to contextually appropriate English translations. – This task could be made harder by choosing a more abstract topic that students will be less familiar with. For example, a B2 text about deforestation might discuss the general trends in your students' country, where deforestation is happening and what are the primary causes. A C1 text, on the other hand, might focus on a particular aspect of deforestation, such as unsustainable forest management.
Variation and extension	– To extend the task, get different pairs to summarise different texts about the same topic. This creates the possibility for an extra stage in which the students combine the information from their separate summaries into a report, article, short talk, etc. – For multilingual groups, the same task could also be done using a text in English, perhaps taken from the coursebook. This sort of summary task could replace the normal reading comprehension task in the book, or it could be a way of revisiting a text seen earlier in the course.
Feedback	This should focus on how well students: a. locate the key points in the source text b. paraphrase these key points and incorporate them into a clear, coherent summary
Adaptation for the virtual classroom	Before putting the students into breakout rooms, the text could be sent to one member of each pair via the chat box in PDF format. Once in breakout rooms, the student with the text then explains the key points to the student who has not read it. Together, they write the summary. This could be done in a shared document and utilising the screen sharing function.

2.3e What should I study?

 About the activity

Mediation task type	Processing text
Mediation strategies	Selecting and omitting information, summarising, paraphrasing
Summary of the activity	Students write an email in which they pass on key points and ideas from an article.

Rationale

In many real-life contexts, we are required to understand the main points and ideas of a text and then pass on this information in a condensed form to someone who has not had the time or opportunity to read the same text.

 How to run the activity

Levels	C1–C2	Learners	Teens/Adults	Time	45–60 minutes

Preparation	Make enough copies of Worksheets A and B so that every student in the class has either A or B. Cut the worksheets along the dotted line.
Procedure	1. Lead into the topic by organising the class into pairs and asking the students to discuss important things to consider when choosing what to study at university. 2. Hand out worksheet A to half the pairs and worksheet B to the other half. 3. Give students time to read the rubric and then ask a few questions to check their understanding of the task, e.g. *Is it important to incorporate ideas from the text into your email?* 4. Students read the text individually. Then, in their pairs, they discuss what information they think would be important to pass on to their friend. 5. Students write their emails individually. Circulate and provide support as necessary. 6. When students finish their emails, create AB pairs. Students exchange their emails and worksheets. Pass out the appropriate peer-feedback form (A or B). 7. Students read their classmates' article and email. They also fill out the peer-feedback form. Students then take turns giving each other feedback. 8. Give general feedback on the task.

2.3e What should I study?

Language	- Reported speech/reporting verbs: *A lot of experts argue that… I'm sure some people will warn you not to…*
	- Lexis related the topic of higher education: *prospective students, ascend a power hierarchy, transferable skills*
	- Functional language for:
	  • Referring to the source text: *from what I've read…, in the article it says…, According to the article…*
	  • Giving advice: *If were in your shoes…, I think the best thing to do is…, I'd suggest…*
	  • Giving opinions: *I have no doubt that…, If you'd like my honest opinion…, My personal opinion is that…*

▼▲ Differentiation	- For some students, assessing is the "teacher's job," so they might not see the value in peer-feedback. In this case, try to "sell" them on the idea. Explain that while assessing their classmates, they are reflecting on how to do the task and this process will help them improve their own skills. - Depending on your group, you might want to consider students doing peer assessment anonymously, for example, by putting a letter or number on their emails instead of their names.
Variation and extension	The writing could be done at home, with peer feedback done at the beginning of the next lesson. If there is time, you could round off the lesson with a general discussion of the topic. Possible questions for this stage could include: - *What priorities should students have when thinking about what to study at university?* - *Is the true purpose of higher education to prepare students for their professional careers?* - *What are the most important skills for university students to develop in order to be successful in both their private and professional lives?* This task could be transformed into a cross-linguistic one by replacing the English source texts with texts on the same topic in the students' L1, or by choosing a text on a different topic and modifying the task instructions accordingly.
Feedback	This should focus on how well students: a. select the key points and ideas in the source text b. paraphrase and incorporate these key points and ideas into their emails c. produce a clearly written, well-organised email in the appropriate register If students include too much extra information, i.e. specific examples or supporting evidence rather than just key points, lead an open class discussion about why it would not be necessary to include this kind of information in a summary.
Adaptation for the virtual classroom	In an asynchronous course, this task could be done using a Learning Management System (LMS), such as Moodle or Blackboard. You could post the materials with clear instructions. The students could then do the task individually and submit their emails through the platform. The discussion board could be used to give general feedback.

2.3e What should I study? – worksheet A

Student A

You have a friend who is having trouble deciding what to study at university. Read the article and write your friend an email (175–200 words) in which you:
- Summarise the main points and ideas
- Give your own opinion on the importance of studying the humanities

Why study the humanities

Humanities is a group of educational disciplines, including the study of languages, history, literature and philosophy, which concern themselves with human beings and their culture. Today, it is common for students, not to mention their parents, to ask, why study the humanities?

In a certain sense, education consists of learning to ask and answer questions. While science does involve a degree of higher-order thinking, such as creativity and critical thinking, in general, the more expert judgement is required to either ask or answer a question, the more likely the question is related to the humanities. For example, it would be impossible to create a scientific way of determining the artistic value of a painting or the morality of a proposed law. To answer these questions, you need good judgement, not mere facts or numbers. Studying the humanities helps you develop this judgement.

The one major criticism levelled at the humanities is that they are impractical. What good is it to study Latin or the French revolution? First of all, ask yourself what really matters in your life. What gives your life meaning? In many, if not most cases, they are activities you do for their own sake. This is exactly what humanists focus on. Not only that, is it not a vital human activity to stop and say, why am I doing this? The importance of the ability to understand, evaluate, and appreciate the ultimate goals for everything we do cannot be understated.

Furthermore, there is also a good argument to be made that the humanities are indeed quite practical. Though scientists of course play a role in the production of today's culture, through the development of new technologies, for example, the people who tend to exert the most influence over our collective consciousness are politicians, journalists, public intellectuals, authors, marketers, policymakers, activists, lawyers and judges. The power these people possess is rooted in their ability to think of new ideas, argue for or against ideas, present ideas in a clear and convincing way.

Instead of questioning the cost and future financial value of humanities degrees, perhaps a better question for students to ask themselves might be: Can I afford not to study the humanities? After all, it is just as important to be a capable, flexible and well-rounded person at work as it is in your private life.

2.3e What should I study? – worksheet B

Student B

You have a friend who is having trouble deciding what to study at university. Read the article and write your friend an email (175–200 words) in which you:
- Summarise the main points and ideas
- Give your own opinion on the importance of studying STEM

Why study STEM

The acronym STEM stands for Science, Technology, Engineering and Mathematics. These academic subjects have received more and more attention in recent years because of their growing importance in today's competitive global economy. There are a number of good reasons for prospective university students to consider a career in STEM.

First of all, studying, and later working, in STEM means living on the cutting edge. Engineers, software developers, computer scientists, chemists – these professionals are finding innovative solutions to real-word problems. People working STEM occupations invented the internet, built the tallest buildings in the world and found cures to the most terrible of diseases. In the modern world, STEM is everywhere. It's in our homes, classrooms and businesses. Studying STEM means, quite literally, building the future we will all inhabit.

In STEM, you will learn transferable skills that are useful in nearly any profession or industry. In fact, recent studies have predicted that up to 75 percent of all jobs will require STEM skills over the next decade. Employees who are good with numbers and data, or have strong technical skills, will be ready to take on any number of roles. Indeed, math, science and programming are universal languages that make possible for teams from around the world to collaborate on difficult problems. In their 21st century skill set, employees need to possess high-level interpersonal, communication, problem solving and critical thinking skills in order to be successful.

STEM is key to the modern economy. So it is perhaps not surprising that STEM graduates are likely to find themselves employed immediately after finishing their studies, in much better paying jobs than those who studied the humanities. When it comes to finding full-time employment, the fields with the best prospects tend to be those requiring STEM skills. A new study found that technology, research, science and engineering jobs will experience more than double the job growth of other fields. The decision to study a STEM subject therefore can make a real difference in terms of socio-economic status throughout your life.

In this new century, it is hard to deny the importance of scientific and technological innovations as we face both the advantages and challenges of globalisation and a knowledge-based economy. To succeed in an information rich and highly technological society, prospective students will need to develop their STEM skills to much higher levels in order to keep up with a world in a constant state of change.

2.3e What should I study? – the peer-feedback forms

Student A peer-feedback form

1. Read your partner's email. Have they included the following main points and ideas? • STEM professionals are involved in important developments that shape the world we all live in. • STEM helps students develop valuable transferable skills. • If you study STEM, you are likely to find a well-paid job rather quickly, which will have long term effects on what type of life you live.	
2. Have they used their own words when they included information from the article?	
3. Have they used an appropriately informal register in their email?	
4. Is the email well-organised and easy to read?	

Student B peer-feedback form

1. Read your partner's email. Have they included the following main points and ideas? • When you study the humanities, you develop good judgement. • In life, activities done for their own sake may not be practical, but they are still very valuable. • The humanities are not as impractical as some people claim, because they help you develop a number of skills that lead to a successful life.	
2. Have they used their own words when they included information from the article?	
3. Have they used an appropriately informal register in their email?	
4. Is the email well-organised and easy to read?	

2.4a Celebrations around the world: Christmas and beyond

 About the activity

Mediation task type	Translating a spoken text in writing
Mediation strategies	Selecting and omitting information, paraphasing, translating, combining, expanding and/or summarising, explaining sociocultural and sociolinguistic elements
Summary of the activity	Students give a rough translation of an informal spoken text in their L1 about what they/people usually do on a celebration/occasion in their country/culture. To do this, they will have to pay particular attention to whether and how to mediate sociocultural and sociolinguistic elements that might be present in the source text – (e.g. traditions, food and drinks, places, as well as typical ways of greeting each other, idioms and sayings).

Rationale

Cross-linguistic mediation tasks provide students with the opportunity to become more skilled in selecting and translating texts in different social contexts, as well as explaining sociocultural and sociolinguistic elements that might be different, the same or not present, in their own or someone else's culture.

 **How to run the activity**

Levels	B1–B2	Learners	Teens/Adults	Time	45–60 minutes

Preparation	– Choose an occasion people usually celebrate in your students' country. This can be a celebration that is more specific to your students' culture, like Hanami in Japan or Chaharshanbe Suri in Iran, or a more "international" one, like Christmas or Easter. – Make a copy of the materials below for each of your students.
Procedure	1. Hand out **A cultural _____** table. Organise class into pairs and explain activity: in pairs, students discuss and fill in the **A cultural _____** table with one or more examples of: – traditions people in their country might follow – the food and drink they might have – the places they might visit or go to – the expressions they might use during this time of year 2. In pairs, students discuss customs in their country on the occasion chosen for the task, and fill in the "**A cultural _____**" table. 3. In open class, have students compare their ideas

2.4a Celebrations around the world: Christmas and beyond

Procedure	4. Organise class into small groups and explain the task: in groups, students have a conversation in their L1 about what they and their family/friends usually do for this special occasion. They have to record their conversations with their smartphones. 5. Students record their conversation in their L1. 6. Ask each group to swap their recording with another group, for example by emailing or texting each other. 7. Explain mediation task: in the same groups, students select and omit information from the recording they've just received to write a short blog post in English of approximately 120-180 words. 8. Hand out **Instructions for mediation task** and have students read the situation: students/bloggers need to decide which information to select or omit from the recorded conversation as well as what information would need extra explaining for a foreign audience. **Note:** Remind your students that they shouldn't translate the recording word for word, but rather select only the most relevant pieces of information from it and use them to write their post. 9. In the same groups, students listen to the recording and select and omit information they want to include in their blog post. Monitor and assist as necessary. 10. Students collaborate in writing the blog post including the information selected in the previous stage. 11. Ask students to swap their blog posts with the group that created the recording in stage 5. 12. Hand out the **Peer-feedback form** and explain the activity: students from each group read the post based on the recording they made in stage 5 and answer the questions in the **Peer-feedback form**. Monitor and assist as necessary. 13. Groups give each other feedback using the **Peer-feedback form**. Monitor and assist as necessary. 14. Give feedback on task.

Language	- Lexis will vary depending on the tradition or celebration chosen: (Christmas) *carols, mistletoe, unwrap, mince pie*.
	- Frequency adverbs and expressions: *Whenever it's (Christmas), we ..., people always/never ... when ..., Every time we (open up our presents)...*
	- Functional language for:
	  • generalising: *Most people..., We usually..., Generally, ..., As a general rule, ...*
	  • contrasting information: *Although people normally ..., our family/I do (wear traditional clothes), instead, in our country, ...*
	  • exemplifying: *for example,..., like, such as, Some of these might be ...*

2.4a Celebrations around the world: Christmas and beyond

▼▲ Differentiation	Some students might not feel comfortable talking about their own ways of celebrating a cultural event as they might not celebrate it in a "traditional" way or at all. Let students decide how to approach the topic and give them the possibility to talk more in general about the celebration you've chosen. For example, they could talk about how people usually celebrate the special occasion in their country/the country they are living in, or how their friends do it.
Variation and extension	- As a follow up activity, you could have students discuss which tradition survives today when people celebrate the occasion chosen for the task, and which ones have begun to fade or have been replaced by more international ones. - With multilingual classes: first, ask your students to individually choose an occasion people usually celebrate in their own country. Then, ask students to record themselves answering the question *What do you and your family/friends usually do on this occasion?* in their L1 using their smartphones. After they have their source text recorded, put the students into pairs and ask them to each play their recording, pause it and translate it for their partners. While students translate their recordings, their partners take notes to write the blog post.
Feedback	This should focus on how well the students have selected/omitted, explained and translated the content of the original text in their L1. Some questions that you could ask yourself while monitoring may be the same as the ones in the **Peer-feedback form** (in the Materials section below). To these, you could also add in the following: - *How well and appropriately have they translated, explained the sociocultural elements from the source text in their L1?* - *What other mediation strategies have they used (e.g. paraphrased, summarised, combined, etc.)? To what effect?*
Adaptation for the virtual classroom	- Do stages 2, 5, 8 and 10 in breakout rooms. - You could run stage 2 as a plenary and have students write their ideas for each category in the chat box.

2.4a Celebrations around the world – the worksheet

1. A cultural _____

Fill in the table below with one or more examples for each of the categories (A–E).

Celebration	*Christmas* (in the UK)	_____ (in _____) celebration/country
A. Traditions people usually follow	• leaving some carrots and water for Rudolph as well as some mince pies and sherry for Santa under the Christmas tree • pulling Christmas crackers	
B. Typical food/drink people have	• mince pies • Christmas pudding	
C. Places people usually go to/visit	• pub • grandma's house	
D. Expressions people often use	• "Christmas keeps coming earlier and earlier." • "Christmas comes but once a year."	

2. Instructions for mediation task

Instructions for mediation task

You run an English-language blog about cultural diversity. In your next post, you've decided to write about what people in your country usually do for a special occasion. To make the post more original, you've interviewed some of your friends and recorded them. Your followers aren't from your country and you want to write about the most cultural aspects of this celebration there, so select only the most relevant information from the conversation and include them in your post.

2.4a Celebrations around the world – the peer-feedback form

3. Peer feedback form

Fill in the form below. Use the lines under each question to write your notes.

Peer-feedback form

1. Is the information included in the blog post relevant and appropriate for a foreign audience?

   ....
   ....
   ....

2. Is everything clear and easy to understand?

   ....
   ....
   ....

3. Are there any points that could be explained better? Which ones?

   ....
   ....
   ....

4. Was anything translated too literally? If so, do you know if these translations are accurate? (If not, search online and confirm).

   ....
   ....
   ....

5. Do you think the writer should make any changes? Why? How?

   ....
   ....
   ....

2.4b Online translation doesn't always work

 About the activity

Mediation task type	Translating a text into speech
Mediation strategies	Selecting and omitting information, paraphrasing, linking to previous knowledge, explaining
Summary of the activity	Students explain the mistakes in an automatic translation into English of a song written in their L1.

Rationale

This task helps students reflect on how to explain in English those sociolinguistic and sociocultural elements that characterise creative texts in their own language.

 How to run the activity

Levels	B2–C1	Learners	Teens/Adults	Time	60 minutes

Preparation	– Use the Internet to find
	  • the lyrics of a song written in your students' L1 (these should include some idiomatic expressions or sayings typical of your students' language/culture)
	  • a reliable translation in English of the song lyrics.
	– Use an online translation tool to translate the song lyrics into English.
	– Print a copy of the original text and a copy of the translated version for each of your students.
	– Make a copy of the worksheet for each of your students.

Procedure	1. Show questions in Activity 1 in the worksheet and tell students they'll discuss them with a partner. Organise class into pairs and hand out the worksheet. 2. In open class, encourage students to share their ideas. 3. Tell students they are going to read the translation into English of a text which was originally written in their own language. While they read the translation, they have to answer the questions in Activity 2. Hand out the translated version of the song lyrics. 4. Students look at the automatic translation and answer the questions in Activity 2. Monitor and assist as necessary. 5. Have students share their answers in open class. 6. Now organise class into new pairs. Tell students to read the situation in Activity 3: in pairs, they have to explain to a foreign friend the parts in the English version of the lyrics that the online translation tool wasn't able to render appropriately.

2.4b Online translation doesn't always work

Procedure	7. In pairs, students select the most inaccurate pieces in the translation and discuss how to best explain these to their foreign friend. 8. Now ask your students to record the voice message for their friend using the voice recorder, a similar application on their smartphones or school's computers, tablets, etc. Monitor and assist as necessary. 9. Ask your students to share their voice message with you (via email, WhatsApp, Bluetooth, etc.) and prepare to give feedback on task.

Language	– Idiomatic expressions: *a dime a dozen, blow your own trumpet, poker face*
	– Sayings: *You can't judge a book by the cover, The apple doesn't fall far from the tree*
	– Functional language for:
	  • refer to the source texts (i.e. original lyrics and the translated version): *Here the subject is missing because in Italian you usually…, The original text says…, In the translated version…*
	  • comparing and contrasting: *In Italian it's… whereas here it says that…, Although the literal translation is correct, in English you would instead say…*

Differentiation	– Some students might struggle with translating or explaining some words, phrases or concepts in English: allow students to use the Internet to check on the meaning and appropriate translations of more challenging expressions. – To add an extra challenge, ask students to try and provide a more "professional" translation into English of the whole song or the most difficult parts.
Variation and extension	– Instead of song lyrics, you could use other genres of creative texts, such as short poems, extracts of short stories and books, etc. – An interesting follow-up activity could focus on the idiomatic expressions found in the creative text in the students' L1 that you've chosen for the task (e.g. song): have students compare these expressions with their English equivalent and discuss the similarities and differences – some might be about animals, while their equivalent in the other language might involve common objects or food, for example. You could also ask them to use the internet to find the origins of the same expressions in English (they'll be surprised to see how some idioms actually had a literal meaning in the past).

Feedback	This should focus on how well the students have explained the mistakes they could find in the translated version of the song to the foreign friend.
	– How well did they explain the inaccuracies in the automatic translation?
	– Were they able to use any English equivalent for expressions in their L1? If they weren't, what other mediation strategies did they use? For example
	  • Paraphrasing
	  • Linking to interlocutor's previous knowledge

Adaptation for the virtual classroom	Set up a class journal folder and share it with your students. Encourage them to write their reflections on sociocultural topics. After this class, for example, they could write about the different idiomatic expressions they've met in the song written in their language, and a brief note with the explanation or equivalent in English.

2.4b Online translation doesn't always work – the worksheet

Activity 1
With a partner, discuss the following questions.
1. How often do you use automatic online translators like?
2. What do you use them for?
3. How reliable do you think they are?
4. Do you think there will be no need for human translation one day?
5. What type of texts do you think automatic translators might be good or bad at translating?

Activity 2
You're going to read the automatic translation in English of a text originally written in your language. For each text, decide:
1. the type of text (e.g. article, poem, review, etc.)
2. why someone might need or want a translation of it (e.g. for homework, a presentation, personal knowledge, etc.)
3. whether it is easy or difficult to read and why

Activity 3
Your foreign friend has just started learning your language. She likes the song and would like to understand what the lyrics mean. She translates them into English using an online translation tool, but she says there are some parts that don't make sense. Select the parts that are difficult to understand and then explain them in a voice message to your friend in English.

Difficult parts

2.4c Lost property

About the activity

Mediation task type	Translating a written text in speech
Mediation strategies	Selecting and omitting information, summarising, paraphrasing, translating, explaining
Summary of the activity	Students give a rough translation into English of one or a series of informative texts in their L1 to help a foreign visitor understand how to deal with lost property.

Rationale

Moving from one language to another has become a necessary and common activity: we often find ourselves in situations where we need or want to help others by translating a text for them, be it a list of the school library rules for a foreign student or administrative procedures to help a foreign visitor.

How to run the activity

Levels	A2–B1	Learners	Teens/Adults	Time	45 minutes

Preparation	Find official websites (e.g. police, public transport companies, governmental agencies, etc.) in your students' L1 that give information on how to deal with/report lost property in their country. Choose one or a series of links to these websites and prepare to share them with your students.
Procedure	1. Lead into the topic by asking students whether they've ever lost property in a public place, where it happened and what they did. 2. Explain situation: students imagine they have just received a call from a foreign friend who's on a road trip around their country. The friend says she's lost her passport somewhere and doesn't know what to do. To help the friend, they decide to do a quick search online and send them a short audio message explaining what they have to do. 3. Share the link/s you've selected for the task with your students and explain task: in pairs, students identify information on how to deal with lost property in their country using the link/s that you've shared with them. They then translate it in an audio message in English for a foreign visitor. 4. In pairs, students use links to official websites to find relevant information in their L1 and make notes on what to include in their audio message. Monitor and assist as necessary.

2.4c Lost property

Procedure	5. Pairs share audio messages with you and the rest of the class – either via Bluetooth, text message or email. They listen to them and prepare to vote for the best solution/explanation. 6. In a plenary, students vote for the best solution/explanation and give reasons for their votes. 7. Give feedback on the task.

Language	- Lexis to talk about lost property: *(fill in/out a) form, keep an item, help desk, lost and found/lost property office*
	- Modals to recommend or suggest: *could, have to, need to, should*
	- Functional language to
	  • organise information: *first, call the …, then, send a copy of …, before going to the police, take…*
	  • explain when translating: *This is what they call… here, This means…, In English, that would be…*

▼▲ Differentiation	Some students might find translating certain terms daunting. Either pre-teach or provide them with the translation in English of the most useful words (e.g. lost and found, form, items, ID, etc.) before they start the task.
Variation and extension	- Instead of translating, students could be presented with source information in English and asked to explain the most important points to someone with a limited proficiency of English. In this case, the task would focus on developing students' ability to relay specific information in speech. - Students could be asked to find the information on their own at home before coming to class and prepare to explain it in English, for example, translating the keywords from the texts they've found. In class, they could then do the task and record their voice message.
Feedback	This should focus on how relevant and concise the content transferred from the text/s in their L1 is in their audio messages: - *Did they select the most relevant key points? (Are the steps relayed useful for the foreign friend?).* - *Is the audio message (the steps in the procedure) clear? Are there any points that need better/further clarifying?* - *What strategies did they use to make up for their lack of more technical/ specialised vocabulary (e.g. did they explain, paraphrase, use examples, etc.)?*
Adaptation for the virtual classroom	To demonstrate the activity (either when giving instructions for the task in stage 2 or to show them an example) you could share your screen and visit the lost property or police office website. Explain as you navigate the website.

2.4d What's on the menu?

 About the activity

Mediation task type	Translating a written text in speech
Mediation strategies	Translating, linking to previous knowledge, explaining
Summary of the activity	Students perform a roleplay in which one person helps a friend understand the contents of a menu in a language they do not understand.

Rationale

People who speak more than one language will find this situation very familiar, perhaps when they are living abroad and friends or family members come to visit. This task gives students valuable practice mediating between their L1 and English in this common real-life situation.

 How to run the activity

Levels	A2–B1	Learners	Teens/Adults	Time	30 minutes

Preparation	– For monolingual groups, find or create a few different menus in the students' L1. It's best if the menus reflect traditional food from the students' home country. If your group includes learners from various language backgrounds, ask them to find or create a menu in their L1 for homework and bring it to class. Note that most restaurants nowadays have downloadable menus available online. – Make a list of useful language (see language section below). This could be put up on the board or on a worksheet.
Procedure	1. Lead into the topic, perhaps by asking what traditional dishes they would recommend to friends from other cities, countries or cultures, and explain the situation: *You would like a foreign friend to experience a traditional meal from your country, but when you get to the restaurant, the menu is only in your language.* 2. Consider modelling an explanation of a dish on one of the menus, incorporating some of the useful language from your pre-prepared list, i.e. *it's made of, it's fried in*. You could model two versions, one with too much information and another one that is clearer and more succinct. Then ask students why one might be better than the other. 3. Organise the class into pairs/small groups. Students perform their roleplays. These should include explanations of some, but not necessarily all, of the dishes on the menu. Make sure students include the type of clarifying questions a foreign friend would be likely to ask. Monitor and provide support where needed. 4. Give feedback on the task.

2.4d What's on the menu?

Language	- Describing unfamiliar food or cooking-related concepts: *It's a type of, It's made of/with, Normally, this food is associated with (weddings, Easter)*, etc. - Encouraging/warning: *If you (don't) like… you will (won't)…, I'm sure you'd love…* - Clarifying: *I'm not sure I understand., Do you mean..?, Is it similar to..?* - Food related lexis: *starter, first/second course*
▼▲ Differentiation	The task could be made more challenging by choosing (or creating) a menu with a wider variety of items, or by including more complex dishes. Students could also be given time to prepare at home before class. To scaffold the roleplay a bit more, students could write out the dialogue before performing it.
Variation and extension	For multilingual groups, students could find a menu in their own L1 and explain the dishes to a student from a different language background. Note that this task lends itself well to task repetition. Students can switch roles and/or groups and repeat the task with a different menu.
Feedback	Peer and teacher-led feedback should focus on how clear the explanation was, how well any doubts were resolved, and so on – in other words, how successful the students were in making the content of the menu accessible to their "foreign" friend.
Adaptation for the virtual classroom	The roleplays could be carried out in breakout rooms. If students have found a menu online or taken a photo of one, or even created a menu themselves for homework, during the roleplay, they can show it to their classmates with the screen sharing function.

2.4e Signs and notices

About the activity

Mediation task type	Translating a written text in speech
Mediation strategies	Paraphrasing, translating, explaining
Summary of the activity	Students perform a roleplay in which they practise giving a rough, spoken translation of signs and notices to a visitor who does not speak the local language.

Rationale

This activity gives students valuable practice providing an approximate translation in common real-life situations.

How to run the activity

Levels	A1–A2	Learners	Teens/Adults	Time	20 minutes

Preparation	Take pictures of various signs or notices in the students' first language. These can also be found quite easily by doing an online search. Note that the signs should include some text and not just icons. Print out a set of these images for each pair of students.

Procedure	1. Lead into the activity by asking students to imagine they are visiting a place where they don't speak the local language. Brainstorm situations where it might be necessary to ask a local for help understanding a sign or notice, e.g. at airports, museums, shops, etc.
	
	2. Explain the activity: students are going to do a roleplay in which Student A is a visitor who doesn't know the local language and Student B is a local. Student A asks Student B for help understanding simple signs and notices in the local language.
	
	3. In open class, choose one example of a sign or notice and model the activity with a stronger student, who is in the role of the visitor. For example:
	
	    Student A: "Sorry I need some help. What does this say?"
	    Student B: "It says you can only pay in cash."
	    Student A: "Okay, thank you."
	
	4. Organise the students into pairs. Give Student A in each group a set of signs and notices. Ask them to roleplay a simple interaction for each one.
	
	5. While students perform the roleplay, go around the class and provide support as necessary. Note that students should try to translate the signs or notices to the best of their ability without too much help from the teacher, even if they don't know an important word. This will help them develop valuable mediation strategies, such as paraphrasing, giving examples, etc.

2.4e Signs and notices

Procedure	6. After a few minutes, ask students to switch roles, with Student A now in the role of the local and Student B in the role of the visitor. 7. Round off the activity in open class by asking if any of the signs or notices were more difficult to translate than others, and, if so, why. 8. Give feedback on the task.

Language	- Lexis related to signs: *gift shop, on sale, price, opening times*
	- Modals for ability: *You can't park here… You can buy souvenirs near …*
	- Functional language for:
	  • Asking for help: *Can you help me? Sorry. Excuse me.*
	  • Expressing gratitude: *Thanks for… Thank you very much.*
	  • Referring to the source text: *The sign says… This word here means… Here it says…*

▼▲ Differentiation	- A1 students could do the lead-in and final feedback stage in their L1. - You may need to provide some language support for students to successfully perform the task, because certain words may be too hard for them to paraphrase. For each sign or notice, you could provide the translation of a few keywords on the worksheets. - To help shyer students gain confidence, they could write out the dialogues before performing them.
Variation and extension	- Instead of finding the examples of signs and notices yourself, you could explain the activity and then have your students find some of them for homework. For multilingual classes, students could find examples of signs and notices in their first language. - After receiving feedback on their roleplay, students could switch partners and repeat the task with the same or different signs and notices.
Feedback	This should focus on how well students were able to use their available linguistic and paralinguistic resources to translate the important message or information contained in the sign or notice, as well as how well they were able to employ appropriate mediation strategies. In an optional reflection stage, students could discuss the following questions (in English or their L1): > - How clear and easy to understand were your partner's translations? > - What strategies did you use when you didn't know a specific word? How successful were you? > - Do you think you could do this type of translation activity in real life? Why or why not? © DELTA Publishing, 2021 | www.deltapublishing.co.uk ACTIVITIES FOR MEDIATION ISBN 978-3-12-501744-3 by Riccardo Chiappini and Ethan Mansur
Adaptation for the virtual classroom	The roleplays could be done in breakout rooms. Beforehand, send the signs and notices in a PDF format through the chat box. While monitoring, you may want to consider entering the breakout rooms with your camera and audio off in order to be as unobtrusive as possible. If the students ask for help with specific vocabulary, type it into the chat box so they can refer to it later. While in breakout rooms, encourage students to use the "ask for help" button (if available in your video conferencing application) when they need assistance.

2.4f *SOS* SMS

 About the activity

Mediation task type	Translating a written text in writing
Mediation strategies	Selecting and omitting information, summarising, paraphrasing, translating, explaining
Summary of the activity	Students translate short text messages in their L1 into English to help a foreigner understand them.

Rationale

It's not always easy to tell if a text message you receive in a language you don't understand very well is actually important or just an advert from your mobile phone provider. In this situation, it can be very useful to have the help of someone who does know the local language.

 How to run the activity

Levels	A1–A2	Learners	Teens/Adults	Time	20 minutes

Preparation	Find examples of both important and unimportant text messages in your students' L1 that phone and internet providers or other companies in your students' country might send their clients or potential clients. For example: IMPORTANT: getting close to calls or data limit, voicemail notification, late delivery of a parcel, etc. UNIMPORTANT/DANGEROUS: seasonal discounts; new product available; spam with links to uncertified sources, etc. Put at least three to five text messages together in a document and make a copy of it for each of your students.

2.4f SOS SMS

Procedure	1. Lead into the topic by asking students what types of text messages or emails they receive from their phone or internet provider or other companies in their country. 2. Hand out your selection of text messages or emails and explain the situation: students imagine that a foreign visitor has asked for their help. The foreign visitor has received some text messages in your language but she doesn't understand them. She needs to know whether the text messages are important or not and what the important ones say. 3. Organise the class into pairs and explain mediation task: students read the text messages in their L1. They then briefly explain why the unimportant messages are not worth paying attention to and translate the important ones to the foreign visitor. 4. Before students do the task, use a couple of extra text messages to demonstrate the activity – show or write them on the board and explain: e.g. *This is an advert from an internet provider. It's about a discount for new customers. This one, though, is very important. It's about a product you ordered and says that they will deliver it next Saturday between 9AM and 12AM.* **Note:** Remind students that, as you've demonstrated, they are not expected to "literally" translate the content of the text messages, but rather use their own words to explain them. 5. In pairs, students read the text messages and prepare to explain their content to the foreign visitor in English. Monitor and assist as necessary. 6. Divide the class into AB pairs: students A are the visitors whereas students B are the translators. Students roleplay situation. 7. Reverse roles and mix up pairs so that students don't take the same role twice, if possible. 8. In a plenary, have students discuss what they found challenging, share their doubts about the translation of certain words or concepts from their L1 into English, etc. 9. Give feedback on the task.
Language	– Lexis will depend on the topic/subject of the text messages/emails selected for the task – e.g. text message from phone and internet provider: *three months free, run out of megas, use your minutes* – Present and past simple to explain: *Here they say that…, They're changing the terms of…, They sent this text because…,* – Functional language to 　• deduce: *maybe, perhaps, it's possible that…* 　• suggest: *If you want, you can…, It's (not) a good idea to…, Remember to…*

2.4f SOS SMS

▼▲ Differentiation	Some students might not be familiar with technical words (also in their own language). In case this happens, pre-teach a selection of the most important ones before stage 2.
Variation and extension	Relaying specific information (in speech): with multilingual groups, you could present students with a selection of text messages/emails in English and ask them to relay their content to a friend with a lower English proficiency level. This can also be done with monolingual groups, where students could each get separate messages and then report back to the class on them.
Feedback	This should focus on how well students have relayed the information in their L1 to the foreign visitor using their words in English: - *Have they briefly explained why some texts are not worth talking about?* - *Have they explained the information in the important text messages clearly?* - *Are there any points that they haven't included or that they could have clarified better?* - *What strategies have students used to make up for their lack of more technical/specialised vocabulary (e.g. have they explained, paraphrased, used examples, etc.)?*
Adaptation for the virtual classroom	- Share the document with your selection of text messages/emails with your students before sending them into their breakout rooms (stage 4). - For stage 7, you can ask your students to do a quick search online and find out how to better translate and/or explain a particular word or concept from their language into English.

2.4g Troubleshooting

💡 About the activity

Mediation task type	Relaying specific information in speech
Mediation strategies	Selecting and omitting information, summarising, paraphrasing, adapting language
Summary of the activity	In this jigsaw roleplay, students act out both the roles of the mediator and the person asking for help in different situations.

Rationale

This activity raises students' awareness of the concept of "barriers" in mediation. To overcome these, students in the role of the mediator will have to adapt their communication strategies according to their target audience's background and linguistic knowledge.

▶ How to run the activity

Levels	B1–B2	Learners	Teens/Adults	Time	45 minutes

Preparation	Make a copy of **Worksheet A** for half your students, and a copy of **Worksheet B** for the other half.
Procedure	1. Lead into the topic by asking students what they do when they have trouble with their computer or mobile phone (e.g. who they ask or where they look for help, etc). 2. Explain jigsaw mediation roleplay: students act out two different roleplay situations taking both the role of mediators and person who needs help. Afterwards, they will reflect on their performance. 3. Organise class into AB pairs and give students their corresponding worksheet (A or B). 4. Ask students to do Activity 1 in their worksheet: Student A, the mediator, reads the roleplay situation and prepares to relay the key information from the blog post in worksheet A. Student B reads the roleplay situation on their worksheet and prepares to act out the role of the person asking for help. Monitor and assist as necessary. **Note:** To help them prepare better for this part, encourage both students A and B to consider who the person asking for help is (e.g. age, level of English, etc), what they might already know as well as what they can or can't understand. 5. Students act out the roleplay situation in Activity 1. Monitor and assist as necessary. 6. Repeat stage 4 and 5 following the instructions for the second roleplay situation in activity 2: Student B is now the mediator and Student A is the person who needs help.

2.4g Troubleshooting

Procedure	7. Hand out the feedback form to all the students. Invite them to reflect on their partners' as well as their own performance by filling in the form. 8. Students give each other feedback and share their reflections on their own performance. 9. In open class, encourage pairs to share some interesting points discussed in the feedback stage. 10. Give feedback on the task.
Language	Lexis to talk about troubleshooting with electrical devices: *hold the home button, tap on outgoing mail server, install key cartridges, print wirelessly, etc.* Functional language to – express cause: *to delete the email accounts, go to…, if you want to connect it by cable, then you…* – explain: *"tap on the icon" means…, the internet service provider is the company that…,* etc. – suggest and recommend: *you have to reset your phone, you could use the cable to start the connection, then…,* etc.
▼▲ Differentiation	Some students might feel uncomfortable acting (or find it difficult to act) out the role of the person asking for help. You could first model the person with limited knowledge of technology (Activity 1) or proficiency of English (Activity 2) could say, giving them ideas about or examples of what to pretend they don't know or understand.
Variation and extension	– As an alternative lead-in, tell your students about some troubleshooting you might have recently had to deal with, either with your phone or other electrical devices. Then, invite your students to ask you questions and/or talk about their own experiences. – To make the task cross-linguistic, find problems and solutions in blogs written in your students' L1. Also, remember to tweak the situations accordingly: for example, the flatmate in Activity 2 could have recently moved to your students' country, so the instructions are only in your students' L1. Students will then read the suggested solutions to the problem in their first language and then relay the key points in English.
Feedback	This should focus on how well the students in the role of the mediator have relayed the information from the source text, taking into account the linguistic and/or knowledge barriers of their target audience. The mediation strategies to look out for here are: – summarising – explaining – adapting language – linking to interlocutor's previous knowledge
Adaptation for the virtual classroom	Have students prepare for the roleplays in individual breakout rooms. This will allow you to provide them with all the personalised assistance they need to perform the different situations.

2.4g Troubleshooting – worksheet A

Activity 1

The situation

Your elderly neighbour has asked you to help her solve a problem with her phone. She tells you that her grandson gave her his old smartphone and that since she started using it, a strange message has been appearing on her display. The message reads "Cannot verify server identity". She also tells you that the only things she can do on her smartphone is make and receive calls, and read and send text messages.

Read the information below that you've found on a blog and prepare to explain to your elderly neighbour how to solve the issue.

CleverB97 – Does anyone know how to make the "Cannot verify server identity" message disappear from my phone???

RAGNARØK – I've had the same problem. I tried to tap on the only option given in the message ("Okay") but that didn't solve it. After lots of trouble, here are the steps I followed to make the message finally disappear for good:

1) Go to "Settings" and find "Mail". In Mail, click on your email address and tap on "Outgoing Mail Server". Delete the server!
2) If you have more than one email address on your phone, repeat stage 1 for each of the other addresses.
3) Go back to "Mail" and add back your email account (or accounts if you have more than one)
4) The "Cannot verify server identity" message will pop up again. This time, though, instead of only one option ("Okay"), you'll have two ("Okay" and "Continue"). Tap on "Continue".
5) You'll be asked to verify the server, so click on "Trust Certificate".
6) Problem solved!

Just send me a private message here on the blog if you have any more questions.

Activity 2

The situation

You're Italian. You've just moved to the UK and your level of English is still quite low. You've just bought a new printer from a local shop and the instructions are only in English. You want to connect your new printer to the Wi-Fi network in your new flat, but you don't understand the instructions well. For this, you've asked your flatmate to help you. Prepare to roleplay this part.

2.4g Troubleshooting – worksheet B

Activity 1

The situation

You are 67 years old. Your grandson has recently given you his old smartphone. For the past few days, a strange message keeps appearing on your phone's display. The message reads "Cannot verify server identity". You keep tapping on "Okay" to make the message disappear, but it continues coming up. Since the only things you can do on this new smartphone is make and receive calls and read and send text messages, you have asked your friendly neighbour to help you solve the problem! Prepare to roleplay this part.

Activity 2

The situation

Your Italian flatmate has just bought a new printer. He says he wants to connect the printer to the Wi-Fi, but the instructions are only in English. He says he's already tried looking for the information on the internet, but he can't find information in Italian for the same brand. His level of English is still quite low so he asks you to help him understand what the instructions say. Although his English is not very good, you know that your friend already knows how to use a computer.

Read the information below and prepare to explain to your flatmate how to connect the printer to the Wi-Fi.

Connect printer to Wi-Fi network

To wirelessly print, connect your printer to your local Wi-Fi network. This must be the same network as the one on your computer or any other device from which you want to print. (Follow the same steps if you changed your internet service provider or if you have installed a new router and need to reconnect your printer).

On the touchscreen control panel of your printer:

1. Enter the **printer code** (8-digit number on the back of the printer)
2. Place the printer near the Wi-Fi router
3. Before turning on the printer, install ink cartridges and load paper in the main tray
4. Tap on **Wi-Fi**, then on "**Settings**" and finally on "**Wireless**"
5. Select your network name and type in the password.

If you cannot find your network name in the list in **Wireless**, go to **Restore Network** and click on **Restore**.

If you still cannot see your network name in the list in **Wireless**: go to **Network Settings** (or similar), enter the network name manually and then type in the password.

2.4g Troubleshooting – the feedback form

1. Answer the questions below.

Questions	Your answers
1. What did you like most about your partner's performance as mediator? What do you think your partner could have done better to play this role?	
2. What did you like most about your partner's performance as the person asking for help? What do you think your partner could have done better to play this role?	
3. How difficult was it for you to play the role of mediator? Why do you think so?	
4. How difficult was it for you to play the role of the person asking for help? Why do you think so?	
5. What did you like most about your performance as mediator and person asking for help? What do you think you could have done better to play these roles?	

2. Now share your answers with your partner. Do you agree?

2.5a Breaking news

 About the activity

Mediation task type	Expressing a personal response to a creative text (including literature)
Mediation strategies	Selecting and omitting information, summarising
Summary of the activity	Students watch a short clip from a film or TV series, and then they retell the event in the form of a news story for a radio programme. One good option could be the Hogwarts letter scene from the first Harry Potter film.
Materials	• A short video clip of your choice • Mobile devices to record with

Rationale

This activity will give students valuable practice with mediation strategies we commonly use to retell interesting events we have witnessed first-hand or ones we have seen in films or TV series.

 How to run the activity

Levels	B2–C1	Learners	Primary/Teens/Adults	Time	45–60 minutes

Preparation	– Find an appropriate clip from a film or TV series. Make sure that something "happens" in the clip that could be reported on, and that it's not just dialogue. – At least half the students will need a mobile phone or tablet with a voice recorder. – Make enough copies of the worksheet for each student in the class.
Procedure	1. Lead into the activity by asking what kind of information is important to include in news stories. Explain that when reporters at news organisations think about what information to include in their stories, they often start with the so-called "Five Ws and an H". Give them one of the Ws, for example, *who*, and then try to elicit the other question words. 2. Explain the activity: the students are going to watch a short clip from a film or TV series and take notes on the "Five Ws and an H" of the event. Afterwards, they will act as radio news reporters and create a short radio story based on their notes. They will use their mobile phones or tablets to record the story. 3. Hand out a copy of the worksheet to each student. Students watch the clip and do Activity 1. They then compare notes in pairs or small groups. Play the clip again if necessary.

2.5a Breaking news

Procedure	4. In open class, elicit the important information for each of the "Five Ws and an H" to the board. 5. Students do Activity 2 in pairs or small groups. Afterwards, in open class, you could ask all the students to turn over their worksheets and quiz the whole class. 6. Put the students into new pairs. Together, they decide what to include in their news story, which they will write together. While one student records the radio story, their partner can use their notes as a checklist to make sure nothing important is missed out. Encourage students to record their news story more than once, because they are likely to tell the story fluently after a bit of practice. 7. Tell the students to email you their stories so you can listen to them carefully after class. If time allows, students could listen to each other's stories and vote on their favourite. 8. Give feedback on the task.
Language	– Lexis related to the topic of the clip (for example, the Hogwarts letter scene): *eyewitness, letterbox, front garden* – Passives: *The police were called to a house on Privet Drive after they had received complaints of a large number of owls in the neighbourhood.* – Reported speech: *Local residents said the owls were carrying letters. A young boy told the police his uncle wouldn't give him an important letter.*
Variation and extension	– The news report could instead be an interview, where a reporter interviews an eyewitness to a newsworthy event. – Your students could also retell the events in the form of a written news story.
Feedback	This should focus on how well the students were able to retell key elements of the event using the appropriate register and structure of a radio news story. In an optional peer-feedback stage, students could listen to their classmates' news stories and reflect on the following questions: – How well was your partner able to retell the story? – Is the news story clear and easy to follow? – Was anything important left out? – What made the task challenging? Why? How were you able to overcome these challenges? © DELTA Publishing, 2021 | www.deltapublishing.co.uk ACTIVITIES FOR MEDIATION ISBN 978-3-12-501744-3 by Riccardo Chiappini and Ethan Mansur
Adaptation for the virtual classroom	For asynchronous courses, you could post the film clip on a Learning Management System (LMS), such as Moodle or Blackboard, with clear instructions on how to do the task. Students could then individually record themselves performing the radio news story and upload them to the online platform, where they could be shared with other students and also assessed by the teacher. On the forum, students could reflect on the task, what they found easy or difficult, as well discussing similarities and differences between their stories.

2.5a Breaking news – the worksheet

1 Watch the short clip and take notes.

	Notes
Who is the story about? Identify important people.	
What happened? Identify important events and facts.	
When did the event take place? Identify the time of day, year.	
Where did the event take place? Identify the country, city, etc.	
Why did the event happen? Identify important causes/ reasons.	
How did the event happen? Identify the sequence of events.	

2 Work in pairs. Read the following tips for creating a news story for the radio. Then cover the worksheet and try to remember as many as possible.

1. Start with a brief introduction that will make people want to keep listening.
2. Try to include information about the *who*, *what*, *when*, *where*, *why* and *how* of the event as soon as possible.
3. The structure of a news story is simple: start with general information and then move into more specific details.
4. Don't include personal opinion. Be as objective as possible.
5. Keep your story "short and sweet." On the radio, it's harder to follow long, complicated stories.
6. Include quotations from people who witnessed the event.
7. Finish your news story by stating your name and the city where you are based, for example, *Antonia Liberal Trinidad, Madrid*.

3 Work in pairs. Use the notes from Exercise 1 and record a short news story on your mobile phone or tablet. Follow the advice from Exercise 2.

2.5b Compare and review

 About the activity

Mediation task type	Analysis and criticism of creative texts (including literature)
Mediation strategies	Selecting and omitting information, summarising, combining
Summary of the activity	Students analyse two short animated films focussing on some technical features, such as target audience, plot and characters. Then, based on their analysis, they write a review for an international audience.
Materials	• Worksheet 1 and 2 • Access to the internet/digital devices

Rationale

One important reason to use creative texts in class is for students to learn how to appreciate them. In this activity, students have the opportunity to focus also on more formal aspects of this type of text as well as on how to "criticise" them.

 How to run the activity

Levels	B2–C1	Learners	Teens/Adults	Time	45–60 minutes

Preparation	– Find two short animated films about the same topic, made by the same author or produced by the same studio. You can do your search directly on YouTube by typing, for example, "short animations about friendship", "Ghibli short movies" or "Pixar shorts". – Make sure that at least half of your students have a smartphone or tablet and are able to connect to the internet from the classroom. – Make a copy of the worksheet for each of your students. Print a copy for yourself and fill it in with the answers. Refer to this for feedback.
Procedure	1. Show the titles of the two short animated films you've selected. Elicit your students' reactions and predictions. 2. Fill in Part 1 of Worksheet 1 by finding relevant information on the internet using smartphones or school computers, tablets, etc. 3. In open class, students share the information they've been able to find out on the internet. 4. Allow enough time for students to go through the information and questions in Part 2 of Worksheet 1. Then, students watch the short animated films and fill in each of the sections in Part 2 with their notes. 5. Reorganise the class into different pairs. Students share their opinions/ideas using their notes from the previous stage.

2.5b Compare and review

Procedure	6. Give Worksheet 2 to each of your students and explain the task: Individually, students use their notes to write a review for an international audience in which they compare the two short animated films. 7. (Optional). Students stick their reviews on the walls, read each other's reviews and vote for the best one. 8. Collect reviews and prepare to give feedback on the task.

Language	- Lexis to talk about films: *plot, setting, theme, producer*
	- Evaluative adjectives: *amazing, touching, un-/realistic, stunning*
	- Functional language to
	  • give opinions: *I've thoroughly enjoyed…, I am glad I watched it because…*
	  • suggest and recommend: *Although I enjoyed it, I wouldn't recommend it for…, You should definitely show it to…*

▼▲ Differentiation	- Some students might need more time to complete stage 4. In this case, allow them to watch the shorts once more. - Some students might need more support for them to identify the theme and target audience. Before watching the shorts, give an example with a popular animation or film among your students and elicit the theme and target audience (e.g. Mickey Mouse and the Club House). - Some students might need more time to finish their review. Allow them to write just a draft – which they can still use for the optional stage (stage 7 in the Procedure above) – and then let them finish it at home and hand it in at the next class.
Variation and extension	- Instead of asking students to use the internet in stage 2, provide them with written texts that include the necessary information for them to fill in Part 1 of the worksheet. These could be fact files or printouts from Wikipedia or Rotten Tomatoes entries for the films you've selected. - For students to focus more on the text type "review," they could all write a draft in class and then complete it at home.
Feedback	This should focus on how well the students have combined in their review - their notes from stages 2 and 4 - their own background knowledge (e.g. of the genre, author, etc.) - their personal opinion
Adaptation for the virtual classroom	Use the share-screen function to show the shorts in the main room. For students to watch the videos on their own, set up a shared folder with the video files or send the links to the videos through the chat box.

2.5b Compare and review – worksheet 1

Part 1

Find relevant information on the internet to fill the table below.

Short 1 title:	Short 2 title: ....
AUTHOR e.g. Name, country, awards, other animations, personal life, etc.	
Short 1	
Short 2	
COUNTRY	
Short 1	
Short 2	
RUNNING TIME	
Short 1	
Short 2	
RELEASE DATE/YEAR	
Short 1	
Short 2	

Part 2

Watch the two shorts and fill in the table below.

CHARACTERS Who are they? Do they (their opinion, point of view, etc.) change during the story? How?	
Short 1	
Short 2	
PLOT e.g. Is it clear and easy to follow? Which events/scenes are the most important?	
Short 1	
Short 2	
THEME e.g. What is the main theme? What aspects of the theme does the author focus more on?	
Short 1	
Short 2	
TARGET AUDIENCE e.g. Age, country, likes/interests, etc.	
Short 1	
Short 2	

2.5b Compare and review – worksheet 2

Instructions

REVIEWS WANTED

An international cinema magazine, *Aninema*, has organised a contest for short animation fans. The winners will have their review published in the next issue of the magazine.

To participate, choose two animated shorts you've recently watched and write a review comparing them. In your review, you should include:

- General information for both shorts
- A reflection on the most important elements in each short and how similar to or different from each other they are
- Whether you would recommend watching them and why.

Now, look back at your notes from Part 1 and Part 2 and decide which information to include in your review.

2.5c Film feelings

 About the activity

Mediation task type	Expressing a personal response to creative texts (including literature)
Mediation strategies	Selecting and omitting information, summarising
Summary of the activity	Students make a short video for a film blog in which they describe their emotional response to a favourite film.

Rationale

One common way of engaging with a film is to describe and relate the feelings and emotions we experience while watching it.

 How to run the activity

Levels	B1–B2	Learners	Teens/Adults	Time	45 minutes

Preparation	Make a copy of the worksheet for each student in the group.
Procedure	1. Tell the class that the topic of today's lesson is films. Put the students into pairs. Give them five minutes to discuss the questions in Activity 1. In open class, ask a few students to briefly report what they talked about with their classmates. 3. Students do Activity 2, which provides a variety of adjectives for describing emotions and feelings. Circulate and address any issues related to meaning or pronunciation. 4. In pairs, students do Activity 3. Make sure to give students at least a minute of "thinking time" to prepare their description of how they felt during a specific part of their favourite film. 5. Explain that students will record their videos at home, but they will rehearse in class. Allow students time to prepare individually. Then, in their pairs, students practise what they are going to say in their videos. Encourage the student listening to use the bullet points in Activity 4 as a checklist, to make sure their partner has included all the points from the instructions. Circulate and provide support as necessary. 6. If time allows, put students into new pairs and ask them to rehearse once more. 7. Give feedback on this stage of the task, with the purpose of helping the students improve on their performance when they create the final videos at home. (Look at the feedback section below for ideas about what to focus on when assessing this task.) 8. Students record their videos at home and email them to you. 9. In the following lesson, show a few of the best videos and give general feedback on the final stage of the task.

2.5c Film feelings

Language	- Lexis related to feelings and emotions: *be/feel relieved, get excited, experience a feeling of…* - Film genres: *romance, comedy, action film* - Discourse markers: *and then, at that point, finally* - Verb patterns: *It always makes me smile when… I decided to talk about this scene because…* - Relative clauses: *The main character is a girl who… They live in a town where everyone…* - Present simple and continuous: *The main character is walking through the forest when suddenly a ghost appears…, The suspect is driving fast through the town centre and the police are following him on motorbikes…*
▼▲ Differentiation	- If you think your students might not be familiar with some of the adjectives in Activity 2, you could check their meaning with mime or using pictures from an online search. - If students feel uncomfortable with the idea of recording a video of themselves, give them the option of speaking but not appearing in the video. For example, they could create a PowerPoint presentation with images from the film and use a screen casting programme that records both their voice and their screen while they are talking. - With more outgoing, theatrical students, encourage them to dress up in costumes, use props, act out a scene from the film, appear in interesting locations, design a special background or set, etc. to make their videos more entertaining.
Variation and extension	- Before doing stage 5, you could model the activity by talking about a favourite film of your own. Students could listen and take notes on the three bullet points in Activity 4. You could also pre-record yourself doing the task and show the video. - This mediation task could be easily adapted to the topic of TV shows or fiction books. - With the students' permission, the videos could be posted to a real blog or a social media platform, where the rest of the class could watch and comment on them. In the following lesson, students could vote for different categories: funniest film, best costume, best set design, etc.
Feedback	This should focus on how well students were able to give a brief summary of their film, as well as describing and relating the emotions they experienced while watching it. Questions to guide your individual feedback of the students' videos could include: - *Does the student include all three points from the instructions?* - *How well is the student able to briefly summarise their film?* - *How organised is the video?* - *How well does the student describe their feelings and emotions?* - *How easy is it to follow and understand?*
Adaptation for the virtual classroom	The parts of the task involving pair work could be done in breakout rooms; the open class activities, in the main room.

2.5c Film feelings – the worksheet

1. Work in pairs and discuss.
   - What is your favourite film?
   - What do you like about it?
   - What kind of film is it?
   - Who are the main characters?
   - What happens in the story?

2. Look at the list of adjectives to describe feelings and emotions. Which ones do you experience while watching your favourite film? Compare with another student.

annoyed	relieved	shocked
worried	sad	terrified
happy	delighted	disappointed
surprised	anxious	bored
angry	excited	thrilled
nervous	upset	afraid

3. Work in pairs. Think of a specific point in your favourite film where you experienced one of the emotions listed in Activity 2. Explain why.

4. A film blog has asked its readers to contribute a short video (2–3 minutes) on the topic of "the feelings of film." Record a short video in which you:
   - Give a brief description of the film
   - Talk about emotions or feelings you experience
   - Describe a scene that produces a particularly strong emotion or feeling

2.5d Motives

About the activity

Mediation task type	Expressing a personal response to creative texts (including literature)
Mediation strategies	Selecting and omitting information, summarising
Summary of the activity	Students each choose a different graded reader, which they have two months to read. Then each student gives a short presentation which focuses on the development of one of the main characters.

Rationale

This task encourages students to take advantage of the many benefits of extensive reading, as well as developing valuable mediation skills by exploiting the "information gap" created by all the students reading different books.

How to run the activity

| Levels | B1–B2 | Learners | Teens/Adults | Time | 45 minutes |

Preparation	– Make a copy of the worksheet for each student in the group. – Make a suggested reading list of graded readers that would be appropriate to their level. DELTA Publishing Readers are available on our website: www.deltapublishing.co.uk
Procedure	Class 1 1. Lead into the activity by asking students to think of reasons why reading in English is a good way to improve their language skills. 2. Introduce graded readers, if students are unfamiliar with them. Tell them that they have two weeks to find one they would like to read. If your school doesn't have a library with a good selection, show the students websites, such as www.deltapublishing.co.uk, where they can be bought inexpensively. There is also the possibility of using "virtual libraries." Tell the students that once they find their book, they shouldn't start reading it just yet.

2.5d Motives

Procedure	Class 2 1. Two weeks later, students bring their books to class. Hand out a worksheet to each student and give them time to make notes on the questions in Activity 1 individually. Note that you may need to pre-teach *blurb* and *genre*. 2. Students discuss the questions with a classmate. Conduct brief open class feedback. 3. Explain the task: the class has two months to read their books, after which each student will give a short presentation focusing on the development of one of the main characters in their book. During the presentations, they should pay particular attention to the character's motives. Class 3 1. After two months, set aside a lesson for the students' presentations. Alternatively, you could integrate one or two student presentations per week; these could be arranged as and when students finish their books. The students who are listening each have to write down one thing they liked about the presentation and one question for the presenter. Allow time after each presentation for a short Q & A. 2. Round off the activity by asking the students which of the characters they found most interesting, courageous, irritating, kind/unkind, etc.

Language	- Lexis for describing character traits: *brave, persistent, loyal*
	- Lexis for talking about important events: *turning point, make a big decision, there was no turning back*
	- Future tenses: *I think the two friends will have a falling out.*
	- Modals/semi modals: *The main character has to think quickly… She could either…*
	- Functional language for:
	  • Signposting: *To start, to finish, now I'll move on to…*
	  • Talking about consequences: *This resulted in… As a result…*

▼▲ Differentiation	- If a student chooses a book that they immediately find uninteresting, encourage them to set it aside and find another more appropriate book. - Some students may feel the need to look up every word they don't know. Explain that this is a reading fluency activity and that it's only necessary to look up a word or phrase if it is interfering with their enjoyment of the story.
Variation and extension	- Consider getting students to set weekly reading goals. It could also be motivating to dedicate 5–10 minutes of class time once a week for students to briefly summarise what's happening in their books. - Model the activity for your students and choose a book of your own to read and present. This book might be in English or the students' first language. - As presentation aids, students could create posters or PowerPoint presentations.

2.5d Motives

Feedback	– This should focus on how successfully students are able to identify and explain the motives for the main character's actions and the consequences of those actions, as well as the quality of the overall presentation. Use the questions below to provide students with individual feedback on their presentations. 1. *How organised is the presentation?* 2. *How easy is it to follow and understand?* 3. *How engaging and interesting is the presentation?* 4. *Has the student clearly identified important actions taken by the main character, as well as discussing the motives of the character and the consequences of these actions?* 5. *How clearly and concisely has the student described these motives and consequences?*
Adaptation for the virtual classroom	The presentations could be given in the main room. Students could use the chat box for the Q & A.

2.5d Motives – the worksheet

1. Look at your book, including the title, illustrations, the blurb on the back, etc. Take notes on the following questions.
   - What genre is the book?
   - When and where is it set?
   - What do you think will happen in the story?
   - What do you know about the main character? What would you like to know?
   - In what ways do you think the character might change between the beginning of the story and end?

2. Work in pairs. Discuss the questions in Activity 1 with a classmate.

3. While you read, pay attention to the motives for the main character's actions and the consequences of these actions. Use the table to help you. When you are finished with your book, you are going to give a short presentation about it.

Important action	Motive	Consequence
1		
2		
3		
4		
5		

4. Plan your presentation. Divide it into the following parts:
   a. Introduction
   b. Brief character description – appearance/personality
   c. Important events – motives/consequences
   d. Conclusion

2.5e Tweet me

About the activity

Mediation task type	Expressing a personal response to creative texts (including literature)
Mediation strategies	Summarising
Summary of the activity	In English, students summarise a favourite fiction book in a tweet.

Rationale

In our daily life, we are sometimes expected to give someone a quick summary of creative work, such as a favourite book, in order to give the other person a basic idea of what it is about. A fun way of practising this skill is to ask students to do this in writing with an extremely short word limit.

How to run the activity

Levels	B2–C1	Learners	Teens/Adults	Time	20 minutes

Preparation	Make a copy of the worksheet for each student in the group.
Procedure	1. Organise the class into pairs and lead into the topic by asking them to discuss some of their favourite books in English or their L1. 2. Explain the activity: Individually, students will have to summarise a favourite work of fiction in a tweet. 3. Tell students you will start with a short activity involving examples of books summarised in tweets. Pass out a copy of the worksheet to each student. Give students a few minutes to complete Activity 1 individually or in pairs. (Answers: 1 *Don Quixote*, 2 *Pride and Prejudice*, 3 *One Hundred Years of Solitude*, 4 *War and Peace*, 5 *A Thousand and one Nights*). Point out to students that, due to the short word limit of tweets, it is easier to focus on summarising the book's main themes rather than the plot. 4. Students then complete Activity 2 individually. Go around the class and provide support when appropriate. 5. When finished, give students tape or adhesive putty and ask them to stick their tweets on the walls of the classroom. Students walk around the class and read each other's tweets. 6. Round off the activity with an open class discussion of which books sounded particularly interesting. 7. Give feedback on the task.

2.5e Tweet me

Language	- Lexis related to talking about fictional stories: *main character, in a surprise twist, take place* - Social media language: the use of sentence fragments, symbols like @ and #, when to employ all caps, etc. - Narrative tenses: *The mouse had been happy until a new neighbour arrived.*
▼▲ Differentiation	- Some students may find it challenging to condense a whole book into so few words. In this case, let students write a longer summary, perhaps one that is twice as long as the example tweets in Activity 1. In pairs, they can then help each other shorten their summaries. - You could ask fast finishers to write a second tweet summarising another favourite book.
Variation and extension	- Students could write real tweets and post them on the real social media platform, creating their own hashtag to follow. - Students could also be asked to summarise favourite films, TV shows or even narrative-driven video games in tweets.
Feedback	Teacher-led feedback should focus on how successfully students manage to summarise the important themes and events of their stories. In an optional peer-feedback stage, students could discuss the following questions: - *Did you summarise the most important themes of the book in your tweet?* - *Did you have to leave anything important out due to lack of space?* - *Are the tweets clear and easy to understand?* - *What challenges did you have? What were your solutions?*
Adaptation for the virtual classroom	While students are writing their tweets, you could put them into individual breakout rooms. This would allow you to visit and talk to students who ask for help without distracting the others. When finished, students could write their tweets in the chat box, or even post their summaries on Twitter all using the same hashtag.

2.5e Tweet me – the worksheet

1 Match the tweets below (1–5) to the titles of the stories in the box. There is one extra title.

| A Thousand and one Nights | The Tale of the Genji | Don Quixote | Pride and Prejudice | War and Peace | One Hundred Years of Solitude |

1 In this Spanish classic, a rich middle-aged man, who has read too many tales about @chivalry, goes crazy and believes that he is a real knight. He rides with his squire @Sancho having "adventures." He believes his adventures are real, but everyone else laughs at him. #literaryclassics
💬 99   🔁 34   ♡ 290

2 Should we marry for love or money? @Elizabeth Bennet, the daughter of a country gentleman, meets rich and aristocratic @Fitzwilliam Darcy. At first, she doesn't like him AT ALL, but by the end of the book they fall in love.
#happilyeverafter
💬 17   🔁 77   ♡ 180

3 Both the history of @Macondo, a small town in Columbia, and its founding family, the @Buendias, the book follows seven generations of @Buendias, who all seem to have the SAME names.
A wonderful story full of magic, tragedy, history and so much more. #magicalrealism
💬 15   🔁 27   ♡ 1012

4 The plot focuses on @Napoleon's invasion of Russia in 1812. In this book there are no heroes. Nobody is perfect. People change, sometimes dramatically. A dense but unforgettable work full of rich description and physiological analysis.
#readtherussians
💬 123   🔁 22   ♡ 346

5 This is a beloved collection of Middle Eastern folk tales. To postpone a cruel death, princess @Scheherazade tells story after story to @King Shahryar, night after night, including fairy tales, romances, tragedies, fables and parables.
#Islamicgoldenage
💬 18   🔁 21   ♡ 190

2 Choose a favourite book that you have read in your first language. Summarise the book in a tweet. Write your tweet here!

3 Mediating concepts

3a Black holes

 About the activity

Mediation task type	Collaborating in a group – Collaborating to construct meaning
Mediation strategies	Summarising, paraphrasing, combining, expanding, breaking down complicated information
Summary of the activity	Students gather information on the same topic from different sources and, together, they finally collate the most relevant pieces of information into a poster for the school science exhibition.

Rationale

Be it in class, at work or in their personal lives, students collaborate with peers almost on a daily basis. By focusing on mediation strategies to practise this common activity, students will concentrate more on how to combine their own findings and opinions with those of other members of the group, as well as how to make sensible choices that are appropriate to a specific target audience profile.

 How to run the activity

Levels	A2/B1	Learners	Teens/Adults	Time	60 minutes

Preparation	- Bring to class the materials needed to create the poster (sheets of paper, scissors, glue, etc.) - Print the three texts – one copy of each text (Text 1, Text 2 and Text 3) per group.

Procedure	1. Explain the task: students work in groups to create a poster for the school end-of-term science exhibition that will be open to other students, teachers and parents.
	2. Organise the class into groups of three and assign roles (Student A, B and C). Give each student a different text about a different sub-concept:
	  - *Text 1:* "physical properties" of black holes
	  - *Text 2:* "event horizon"
	  - *Text 3:* "gravitational singularity"
	  Note: If you have even-numbered groups, two students can be assigned the same role and work together on the same text.
	3. Individually, Student A, B and C identify key information in their assigned text and prepare to explain the content to their peers.

3a Black holes

Procedure	4. Students relay the key information extracted from their texts to group members.
	
	5. Students combine the key points, which have been selected from each text and agreed upon during the previous stages into their poster. Through this final product they can finally explain to their audience the macro concept "black hole", which they have co-constructed by combining different sub-concepts, i.e. physical properties and structure, event horizon, singularity.
	
	6. In open class, students compare and make notes of similarities and differences between their posters, focusing on, for example, which key points each group has included or left out, how they were combined in the poster, etc.
	
	7. Individually, students reflect on their performance – both as a group and as individual members of the group – by answering questions such as:
	   - *How well do you think you/your partner explained the information in the text?*
	   - *What challenges did you/your partner find when explaining their concept?*
	   - *What can you/your partner do to avoid these challenges next time?*
	
	8. Give feedback on the task.

Language	- Lexis connected to physics and astronomy: *gravity, mass, particles, spacetime.*
	- Passive voice and conditional: *The perimeter of a black hole can be measured by…, If an astronaut ventured too close to a black hole, he/she would be sucked in and pulled apart by the overpowering gravity…*
	- Functional language to
	  • ask for clarification: *Could you repeat what you just said?*
	  • summarise points made during the conversation: *As we said before…*
	  • explain: *Which means…*
	  • paraphrase *In other words…*

▼▲ Differentiation	- (Stage 5) Older/higher-level students should be encouraged to "verbalise" their collaboration further by, for example, asking and answering questions to each other to check understanding or fill potential gaps, summarising points made by other group members or even making sure everyone is on task or receives enough help from the other members of the group to get back on track. - Younger/lower-level students could prepare for the task in advance by reading (listening to or watching) the materials before class.

3a Black holes

Variation and extension	- Instead of a poster for a science exhibition, students could write an article or essay for the school magazine, make a video for a blog about space, or even create a picture book for children. - This activity could also be easily adapted for the higher-primary and lower-secondary CLIL classrooms. The topic (black holes) lends itself to both age groups, but the texts would need adapting. - Groups could be assigned different "macro concepts" to create their posters: For example, one group could work on "black holes" using the same texts as the ones proposed in this task, another group could work on the concept of "sound" in music, and a third one could learn about the notion of "time" in different cultures. In this case, the source texts will need to be replaced by different ones about other appropriate "sub-concepts": to build on the concept of "sound" in music, for example, one student could read about "timbre", another student could read about "pitch" and a third one could read about "intensity". - Instead of using the three texts proposed in this task, students can do research on the assigned sub-concept on their own (either at home or in class). In this case, they could be given the freedom to decide which language to use for their research. On top of being a natural and ordinary activity, sometimes certain information might be "more" available in the students' first language (or in other languages they know) than the target language they are learning.
Feedback	This should focus on how well the students have collaborated to create the poster. Some questions that teachers could answer while monitoring may be: - *To what extent have the students participated and contributed in group work?* - *How well have they passed on the information from their own source text to their peers?* - *Is this reflected in the final product/the poster?* - *How well have they combined their ideas in the poster?* - *Is the information relayed clear and appropriate for the target audience?* Students could also be asked to reflect on their contributions: - *How did you like collaborating in group?* - *What went particularly well?* - *What should you work on as a group?* - *What should you work on yourself?*
Adaptation for the virtual classroom	Students can do stages 4 and 5 in breakout rooms: they could relay the information identified in their own texts and create their poster on a slide (shared through a document collaboration platform). They will then be invited back into the main room to present their poster to the rest of the class (stage 6).

3a Black holes – cards

TEXT 1

What are black holes?

Black holes are very special objects in the universe. Differently from all the planets and stars we know, black holes are actually empty. Almost empty, to be exact. A black hole is a region of space where matter has **collapsed** in on itself, concentrating a huge amount of **mass** at its centre. Here, space is extremely small, but gravity is so great that not even light can escape. Dark and scary, right?

Well, they also look "cool". Some are surrounded by rings like Saturn – called "accretion disks". When the accretion disk moves quickly around the black hole, it becomes extremely hot and it gives off X-rays.

Black holes form when supermassive stars collapse at the end of their life cycle. After a black hole is born, it continues to grow, **absorbing** mass around it, and all this mass collapses into an area that is only some kilometres wide. As for their size, black holes can be as small as a city or as huge as 100,000 times the mass of our sun. Yes, that's "really" big.

And there are definitely many of them. Astronomers say that it is possible that there is a supermassive black hole at the centre of each galaxy. There are 100 billion galaxies in the universe that we know of. That's a lot of black holes.

GLOSSARY

- absorb: to take in liquids, mass or other substance, in a gradual way
- collapse: fall down, fall in quickly and unexpectedly
- mass: a large quantity of substance that does not have a shape or form

---

TEXT 2

The "event horizon"

An event horizon is the part of a black hole from which no object nor light can escape. Light that was **emitted** from inside the event horizon could never reach an observer outside the event horizon. If the same observer saw an object fall into a black hole, it would look like the object was stuck at the event horizon forever.

The reason this happens is because the **gravitational pull** of a black hole is so strong that time slows down around it, making it look like the object will take an infinite amount of time to reach it.

The term "event horizon" – **coined** by Austrian physicist Wolfgang Rindler – indicates that it is impossible to observe any event taking place inside it. The event horizon effectively hides the singularity at the centre of the black hole, making it extremely difficult – if not impossible – for astronomers to make faster progress.

GLOSSARY

- coin (a term or name): invent a new name for something
- emit: send out light, heat, sound, etc.
- gravitational pull: the force a black hole has to attract other objects/materials

3a Black holes – cards

TEXT 3

"Gravitational singularity" of a black hole

Interviewer: **They say that black holes are made from *warped* space and time. What does that mean?**

Scientist: It means that space and time are deformed, completely different from space and time as we know them on Earth and the rest of the universe.

I: **How is that possible?**

Every black hole has a singularity at its centre. If you wanted to measure the **circumference** of a black hole, you would go marching around the black hole and you would see that the circumference is, for example, 30 miles. And then you would try and measure the **diameter**. You would think that the diameter is 30 miles divided by *Pi*, right?

I: **That ought to be 10 miles, more or less.**

S: Yes. But in a black hole the diameter is enormously larger than that – a thousand miles or a million miles. This is what tells us that space is *warped* there.

I: **How can you have a huge diameter in a small circumference?**

S: The answer is simple: all the laws of normal geometry we know just don't apply.

Take a child's trampoline. Put a heavy rock in the centre, and the rock sinks all the way down. That's a black hole. Now, if you were an ant, you would march around the trampoline and have a rough idea of how long its circumference is. But if you marched along the diameter, you would realise that the diameter is much larger than the circumference because you marched down into the centre where the rock is, then back up and out from there. And it's in that very centre where the rock lies that the singularity is: when a star explodes and makes a black hole, that huge mass left from the star remains in the very centre of the black hole: a huge mass in an infinitely small space. Quite "singular", isn't it?

GLOSSARY

- circumference: the line that goes around a circle or other curved shape
- diameter: the line that goes from one side of a circle to the opposite side passing through the centre
- trampoline: rubber sheet for doing jumps in the air for playing or doing exercise

3b Critical incidents

 About the activity

Mediation task type	Leading group work – encouraging conceptual talk
Mediation strategies	Summarising, linking to previous knowledge, explaining, explaining sociocultural elements
Summary of the activity	Students read and reflect on three "critical incidents" – that is real-life stories involving unsuccessful cross-cultural communication. During the discussion, one student takes on a lead role and asks the others to justify their views and reflect more deeply on the topic.

Rationale

In addition to developing students' intercultural competence, this task gives students the opportunity to develop valuable leadership skills.

 How to run the activity

Levels	B2–C1	Learners	Teens/Adults	Time	45 minutes

Preparation	Make enough copies of the worksheet for each student to have one story. Each student in the role of the mediator will also need a copy of the "mediator" card. Cut up the cards.

Procedure	1. Lead into the topic by boarding/displaying the following two brief intercultural encounters. In pairs, students decide if the best answer, in their opinion, is a, b or c. Note there are no "wrong" answers!
	
	   a. Seth asks Jana out on a date. At the end of dinner, Seth asks Jana, "Can we each pay half the bill?"
	
	      a. polite b. neither polite nor impolite c. impolite
	
	   b. Veronica and Nadine are good friends. When Veronica makes mistakes with her English, Nadine corrects her, even in front of other people.
	
	      a. polite b. neither polite nor impolite c. impolite
	
	Discuss the encounters in open class. Elicit that people from different cultures may choose different options, because in different cultures people may have different ideas about what is polite or impolite.

3b Critical incidents

Procedure	2. Tell students they are going to read and discuss three real-life stories that involve unsuccessful communication between people from different cultures. Put the students in pairs. Pass out the cards, with some pairs of students reading A, others reading B, etc. Give them time to read the stories and discuss the questions. Note that these stories involve real people talking about their own personal experiences; they are not meant to represent how all Finnish, Russian or Japanese people would think or behave in these situations. 3. Organise the class into groups of three or four. Each group should include a student who has read each of the three stories. Assign the role of the mediator to one of the students in each group and give them a mediator card. 4. Explain the activity: in their groups, students take turns summarising their stories and reporting what they discussed with their partners during the pair work stage. During this discussion, the mediator will use the questions from their card, as well as any other questions they find appropriate, to encourage students to think more critically about their ideas and opinions, as well as reflecting more deeply on the topic. 5. Round off the activity by asking the students to share any new conclusions they reached during their discussions. 6. Give feedback on the task.

Language	- Lexis related to the topic of critical incidents: *misunderstanding, cause offense, create a moment of confusion*
	- Reported speech/reporting verbs: *My partner convinced me that…, Someone mentioned earlier that…*
	- Conditional sentences: *In this situation, I would have tried to explain that…, If our societies continue to become more and more multicultural…*
	- Functional language for:
	  • Justifying beliefs/opinions: *I think this is true because…, the reason I believe that is…*
	  • Giving examples: *One good example would be… For example…*

▼▲ Differentiation	To support students while they discuss the stories in stage 2, you could provide some of the following cultural background: • <u>Story 1:</u> In Japan, it is considered very disrespectful towards the teacher to eat in class. In the USA, this behaviour is perhaps not encouraged but it is generally tolerated. • <u>Story 2:</u> Competition between students is an important part of the American education system, so students tend to see cheating as unfair or even morally wrong. Russians, on the other hand, tend to think that friends should stick together and help each other no matter what, particularly with any battle with "authority." • <u>Story 3:</u> American culture is significantly less tolerant of silence and spending time alone than Finnish culture. Americans tend to perceive people who are not very communicative as unhappy.

3b Critical incidents

Variation and extension	- An alternative way of leading into the topic would be to tell a personal story involving unsuccessful cross-cultural communication. You could ask the students to reflect on it using the same questions found on the cards. - After the task, students could work in pairs or small groups and brainstorm personal experiences they have had involving unsuccessful cross-cultural communication. They could then choose one to write up collaboratively. These stories could be exchanged with other pairs/groups or put up on the walls of the classrooms. Alternatively, you could regroup students and they could share their stories orally.
Feedback	Feedback for students in the role of the mediator should focus on how well they were able to encourage other group members to: - describe and elaborate on their ideas - justify or clarify their opinions Feedback for other group members should focus on how well they were able to: - contribute their ideas and opinions while at the same time not dominating - build on the contributions of their group mates
Adaptation for the virtual classroom	The lead-in activity could be done as a poll, or answered in the chat box, with the mini intercultural encounters displayed using the screen sharing function. The pair and group work could be done in breakout rooms, but you would have to manually create the groups for the second discussion stage, in order to ensure that each group has students who have discussed each one of the stories.

3b Critical incidents – the worksheet

Student A

Work in pairs. Read the following story and discuss the questions below with a classmate.

Akiko is from Japan. She recently came to the USA to do a master's degree at an American University. On Wednesdays, Akiko is very busy. She has classes all morning and barely any time for lunch. One day she arrived at her Economics class a couple of minutes before it started. She mentioned to one of her American classmates, Carl, that she was hungry because she had been too busy to eat lunch. Just then, the bell rang and the professor started the lesson. Carl opened his backpack and took out a small bag of nuts and a bottle of juice and offered them to Akiko with a smile. Akiko was very surprised and embarrassed. She whispered thank you and refused the offer. Akiko felt even more confused and uncomfortable when she watched Carl open the bag of nuts himself and start to eat them in class. To her complete amazement, the professor did not comment on Carl's behaviour and taught the lesson as if nothing unusual were happening.

1. What do you think motivated Akiko and Carl to act the way they did?
2. What attitudes and values appear to be important to Akiko and Carl?
3. What could Akiko and Carl have done differently to avoid this misunderstanding?

3b Critical incidents – the worksheet

Student B

Work in pairs. Read the following story and discuss the questions below with a classmate.

Yakov is from Russia. He won a scholarship to study for a year at secondary school in the USA. One day during the first term Yakov's French professor announced a pop quiz out of the blue. The quiz was going to be related to the material covered in the last two classes. Yakov was very nervous. He had been busy all that week with an important paper for another course, so he hadn't had time to do his French homework or review what they had done in class. Thankfully, Yakov had a good friend in the class named Allison, who was very keen on French. Allison didn't seem the least bit worried. During the quiz, Yakov asked Allison again and again for the answers to questions he was not sure of, but to his amazement Allison looked really annoyed and refused to help him. She didn't share a single one of her answers. Yakov was very offended. His feelings were hurt. He had thought of Allison as a good friend, but now he felt differently about her.

1. What do you think motivated Yakov and Allison to act the way they did?
2. What attitudes and values appear to be important to Yakov and Allison?
3. What could Yakov and Allison have done differently to avoid this misunderstanding?

3b Critical incidents – the worksheet

Student C

Work in pairs. Read the following story and discuss the questions below with a classmate.

Adda is from Finland. She went to the USA as an exchange student for a year and lived with an American family. She is the kind of person who needs to have some time to herself every day, so in the evening she would go up to her room for a couple of hours and do homework, answer emails or just relax and listen to music. One day her host mother, who wore a serious, worried expression on her face, asked Adda to come sit at the kitchen table. After making them some tea, her host mother started to talk about how it was normal to feel sad and homesick. She began to suggest some activities that she and Adda could do together, so that Adda wouldn't feel so lonely. Adda was very confused. She missed her family, of course, but she didn't feel the least bit sad or homesick. When Adda told her host mother this, however, she didn't seem to believe Adda. Her host mother asked her why she spent so much time in her room. Adda struggled to explain why she liked to spend time alone. It was something she had always done. She had never thought of it as unusual. At the end of the conversation, Adda felt very uncomfortable. She was worried that her host mother now thought she was a bit "strange."

1. What do you think motivated Adda and her host mother to act the way they did?
2. What attitudes and values appear to be important to Adda and her host mother?
3. What could Adda and her host mother have done differently to avoid this misunderstanding?

3b Critical incidents – the worksheet

The Mediator

You are the mediator. Your job is to lead and moderate the discussion.
While you and your classmates discuss the stories, use the following questions (or similar questions of your own) to encourage the group to justify their ideas and opinions and to reflect more deeply on the topic.

1. What do you think might have happened after… ?
2. What reasons do you have for believing that … ?
3. Do you think it is always true that … ?
4. Does everyone in the group agree that … ?
5. Can you give us an example of… ?
6. Can you tell us more about why you think… ?
7. What do you think would happen if…?
8. Do you think it's realistic to think that… ?
9. What can we learn from… ?
10. What can we conclude from our discussion about… ?

3c First day at work

 About the activity

Mediation task type	Leading group work: Managing interaction
Mediation strategies	Summarising, explaining
Summary of the activity	Students roleplay a work situation in which a manager briefs a new employee on their new responsibilities on their first day at work.

Rationale

This activity helps students mediate easy, familiar concepts about their job or field of work. It also encourages them to use questions to check understanding.

 How to run the activity

Levels	A2–B1	Learners	Adults	Time	45 minutes

Preparation	Make two copies of the role cards for each of your students.
Procedure	1. Lead into the topic by asking students to brainstorm a list of things to learn or get used to when you start a new job (e.g. where the photocopier is, login names and passwords, but also how to clean the coffee machine, where to find the helmets, uniforms and so on). 2. Organise the class into pairs: ask students to briefly tell each other about their job, what their main responsibilities are, etc. (Alternatively, ask them to talk about a job they have had in the past or their ideal job). 3. Explain task: students roleplay a situation in which they are managers briefing a new employee on their new responsibilities on their first day at work. The job they are going to explain is the same as the one they have described in stage 2. 4. Students work in the same pairs. Assign roles: Student A is the Manager and Student B is the New employee. 5. Hand out Manager and New employee role cards. Ask Managers and New employees to prepare for the roleplay by filling in section 2 in their role cards: managers fill in the instructions section while new employees complete questions-to-ask section. 6. Students roleplay situation: managers brief new employees and new employees take notes using the table in section 3 in their role card.

3c First day at work

Procedure	7. Once Managers have finished briefing the new employees, New employees ask them questions that have been left unanswered during their explanation, and they answer them. In case managers do not know how to answer a particular question, you can encourage them to make up a sensible answer or simply say that they are not sure and have to consult their own line manager on this. 8. Hand out new role cards and repeat stages 4–8 with Student A acting as the New employee and Student B as the Manager. 9. Give feedback on the task.

Language	– Lexis to talk about work – this will depend on the job each manager will choose. For example: *customer/client, department, timetable*
	– Use of passive voice to talk about tasks and deadlines: *Presentations are given in room 1, This needs to be done/handed in by the end of each week*
	– Functional language to
	  • ask for advice: *Do you think I should…?, Do you think anyone would mind if I…? When is it better to…?*
	  • give advice: *Always/Never…, Be careful (not) to…, It's important to remember that…*

▼▲ Differentiation	Students in lower levels may not know all the vocabulary that is necessary to explain their own job (or a job they've done in the past, etc.) when acting as managers. In this case, run stages 1 to 4 in class. Students can then take the role cards home and prepare better for the roleplay by looking up keywords that they will need to use or explain when briefing the new employees. In the next class, start from stage 5.
Variation and extension	As an extension activity, you could have your students discuss how managers could make employees' first day at work easier and less stressful. At the end, students could even come up with a top-five list of tips for managers to make an employee's first day at work a success.
Feedback	This should focus on how well Managers and New employees have interacted in the roleplay. Some questions that you might find useful when monitoring are: **Managers** – *Have they explained the different aspects of the new job clearly?* – *Have they elaborated on specific points that the New employee has not understood well?* – *What mediation strategies have they employed (e.g. breaking down complicated information, adapting language, linking to previous knowledge)?* **New employees** – *How well have they understood the different aspects of their new job?* – *Did they ask appropriate questions to better understand the key aspects?*
Adaptation for the virtual classroom	Some jobs require the use of certain objects that some students might not be familiar with. For this, encourage Managers to search for images or any other type of visual, and then show them to their partners with the screen sharing function when necessary.

3c First day at work – the role cards

 **Manager**

1. You are the manager. A new employee is starting their new job in your company today. You will have to explain what they have to do. Use the table below to take notes and prepare to brief the new employee.

WHAT tasks they are expected to do in this new job	
WHEN they are expected to do these	
WHERE (1) they will be working	
WHERE (2) to find all the materials that they will need	
HOW they are expected to work and behave	

2. Now explain the information above to the new employee. At the end, encourage them to ask you further questions and ask them questions to make sure they have understood everything.

3c First day at work – the role cards

 **New employee**

1. Your new manager will welcome you and explain what you will do in your new job. First, prepare some questions to ask the manager at the end of their explanation using the table below.

Questions	
WHAT tasks you are expected to do in this new job	
WHEN you are expected to do these	
WHERE (1) you will be working	
WHERE (2) to find all the materials that you will need	
HOW you are expected to work and behave	

2. Now listen to your manager and take notes using the table below. At the end, you will be able to ask them the questions that you have prepared that were not answered by the manager during their explanation.

Briefing	
WHAT tasks you are expected to do in this new job	
WHEN you are expected to do these	
WHERE (1) you will be working	
WHERE (2) to find all the materials that you will need	
HOW you are expected to work and behave	

3d Construction foreman

About the activity

Mediation task type	Leading group work: Managing interaction
Mediation strategies	Summarising, paraphrasing, transforming visual data into verbal text, explaining, combining
Summary of the activity	Students work in groups to build a model.

Rationale

This task gives students the opportunity to reflect on how the success of the team is shaped thanks to the contributions of all the members of a group rather than of one individual.

How to run the activity

| Levels | A2–B1 | Learners | Teens/adults | Time | 45 minutes |

Preparation	Make three/four models using a selection of coloured bricks. Write a set of instructions for each model. Divide the number of pieces of each model by three and put each set in different small bags.
Procedure	1. Explain the task: students work in groups to assemble a model. 2. Organise class into small groups (between three and six students each). Assign roles (e.g. Student A is the Leader; Students B, C, etc. are the Team Members). 3. Give Leaders the instructions for the model their group will have to build. Allow two minutes for Leaders to go through the booklet and memorise the steps as best as they can. In the meantime, give Students B, C and D each a bag with their coloured bricks and ask them to examine them. **Note:** Leaders are not allowed to see what bricks their Team Members have, so encourage the Team Members to hide their bricks, for example, using their empty folders or other objects they have available in class. 4. Set a time limit for groups to assemble the model (e.g. 25 minutes). Then, ask Leaders to quickly brief their Team Members by describing the model their group will have to build. 5. Invite Team Members to take turns and describe their bricks. Remind Team Members that they can describe their bricks but can't show them.

3d Construction foreman

Procedure	6. Leaders start giving instructions to their Team Members: they can ask whether they have a particular brick, call out the next brick to be set, etc. At the same time, the Team Members can interrupt the Leader to ask questions, comment or make suggestions. 7. Once the model is complete, the Leader and their Team Members discuss what went particularly well in addition to what the team could have done better. 8. In open class, students share and comment on the activity. 9. Give feedback on the task.

Language	- Place prepositions: *above, below, beside*
	- Sequencers: *first, afterwards, at the end*
	- Functional language to:
	  • suggest and recommend: *I think this goes on the grey plate, We should build the … first*
	  • ask for repetition: *Can you repeat, please?, What do we have to do when we complete the…?*
	  • reformulate ideas and opinions of others: *In other words…, Like she said…*
	  • combine different contributions: *All of us agree that…, So everyone thinks that…*

▼▲ Differentiation	Some students might have problems describing some bricks: pre-teach vocabulary to help them do this.
Variation and extension	- Instead of assembling models, students could put together puzzles or even order picture stories, comic strips, etc. - Students could record their interaction (stages 4 to 6). For stage 7, ask them to listen to the recording and use it to better evaluate their work.
Feedback	This should focus on how well Leaders and Team members have collaborated to assemble the model. Here are questions you could answer when monitoring the activity: **Leaders** 1. *How well have they described the model (stage 4)? And how well have they explained the different steps to assemble it?* 2. *Have they encouraged their Team Members to comment and suggest? Have they taken these into account?* **Team Members** 1. *How well have they described their bricks?* 2. *How have they contributed in the decision-making process? For example, have they suggested any different course of action while building the model?* 3. *What did they do to improve or repair communication among group members? For example, have they paraphrased what other members have suggested? Have they summarised the Leaders' instructions?*

3d Construction foreman

Adaptation for the virtual classroom	– Instead of working on assembling a model, students could collaborate to create a piece of arts and crafts. The success of the team, in this case, will not depend on the collective efforts of all the Team Members and Leaders to complete one final product, but on each Team Member completing their own version of the same piece of arts and crafts. Another option is to use online jigsaw puzzles (https://www.jigsawplanet.com/): A could share their screen but can only move the pieces that the Team Members (B, C, etc.) describe. – Group-work activities should be done in breakout rooms. Since each Team Member will be working on their own, encourage all Team Members to intervene when they see their colleagues in trouble, or to make a comment or a suggestion for the Leader.

3e DIY word formation

About the activity

Mediation task type	Collaborating in a group: facilitating collaborative interaction with peers
Mediation strategies	Explaining, adapting language, breaking down complicated information
Summary of the activity	In groups, students work together to create their own word formation exam tasks, with each group member focusing on different aspects of the task.

Rationale

By asking students to work in teams to create their own exam tasks, you can help develop their ability to collaborate in a group while at the same time giving them valuable insights into the nature of this particular exam task, how it works in practice and the thinking behind it.

How to run the activity

Levels	B2–C1	Learners	Teens/adults	Time	45–60 minutes

Preparation	- Make a copy of the word formation worksheet. Cut up cards 1–3. - Find one example of a word formation exam task that is relevant and of an appropriate level for your students. Make a sufficient number of copies. Remember to include the answers!
Procedure	1. Lead into the topic by showing students examples of a word formation exam task. Ask them how familiar they are with this type of exam task, whether they find it easy or difficult, what aspects of language are being tested and why, etc. 2. Explain the task: in groups, students are going to create their own word formation exam tasks. Each member of the group will have a different card with important information about how to write this type of task. 3. Put the students into groups of threes. Give each group a copy of an example word formation task to use as a model. Hand out cards 1–3. Note that for groups of four, two students can share a card. Remind students they have to work together to create the exam task, but they are individually responsible for making sure the exam task meets the requirements on their respective cards. 4. Students choose a suitable text of around 150 words to use for their task. These could come from the internet, the coursebook or from print magazines or newspapers. 5. While the students create their tasks, go around and monitor, providing assistance as necessary. Note down specific examples of successful and less successful group work.

3e DIY word formation

Procedure	6. Once the groups have created their tasks, encourage students to double check the information on their cards to make sure they have not missed anything. 7. Organise the class into new groups. The students exchange tasks and complete them. Afterward, give them time to discuss the process of creating them. 8. Give feedback in open class to round off the activity.

Language	- Lexis related to exam tasks: *Answer key, missing words, number of words*
	- Conditional sentences: *Suppose we choose this word. Would it be too difficult to guess? What if we choose this one instead?*
	- Functional language for:
	  • Turn taking: *What do you think? Do you mind if I interrupt? I just want to make one more point.*
	  • Making suggestions: *I think we should…, Maybe it would be better to…*
	  • Establishing common ground: *So it looks like we still need to decide on… Can we agree that we should … ?*

▼▲ Differentiation	If you think your students will have trouble finding a text online, you could give them some suggestions for places to look, for example, using reading texts from sample exams from websites dedicated to exam preparation. You could also simply provide them with a selection of suitable texts to choose from.
Variation and extension	An extra "piloting" stage could be added to step 7. Students get feedback on their tasks from their classmates about, for example, which items were very easy or very difficult, etc. They then go back to their original groups and together decide whether to adjust their tasks according to the feedback they received.
Feedback	This should focus on the quality of the group work, rather than the final product. You might consider how well the groups worked together towards a shared goal, with each participant contributing to the work as required while at the same time not dominating. This task lends itself well to self-evaluation. One idea would be to have students mark themselves from 1–5 (1 needs work, 2 satisfactory, 3 good, 4 very good, 5 excellent) on the following aspects of group work: How well did I … • participate? • contribute ideas? • help keep the group on task? • complete my fair share of the work? • fulfil my specific responsibilities? © DELTA Publishing, 2021 | www.deltapublishing.co.uk ACTIVITIES FOR MEDIATION ISBN 978-3-12-501744-3 by Riccardo Chiappini and Ethan Mansur
Adaptation for the virtual classroom	Introduce and explain the task in the main room and then have the students create their tasks in breakout rooms. Together, the students find a text to adapt on the internet and paste it into a shared document. They then work together to create their word formation tasks.

3e DIY word formation – the tasks

Word formation 1

- The text you use for this task should be about 150 words long. If you include a title, it helps candidates understand what the text is about.
- Remember to provide an answer key, so that you can easily correct the task.
- Make sure the task is not too difficult. The missing words should be relatively easy for your classmates to guess.

Word formation 2

- In the text, use a series of full stops (…………..) to represent the missing words.
- Put a number (1-8) before each missing word.
- For each missing word, you need to put a "stem word" at the end of the line. A "stem word" is a word that has to be changed to form the missing word. For example, if the missing word in the text is "surprising," you could use "surprise" as the stem word.

Word formation 3

- In this task, there are a total of eight missing words in the text.
- There is never more than one missing word per line on the page.
- In a word formation task, there is usually at least one answer that is either negative or plural. For example, if the stem word is "possible," the missing word in the text might be "impossible" or "possibilities."

Word formation 1

- The text you use for this task should be about 150 words long. If you include a title, it helps candidates understand what the text is about.
- Remember to provide an answer key, so that you can easily correct the task.
- Make sure the task is not too difficult. The missing words should be relatively easy for your classmates to guess.

Word formation 2

- In the text, use a series of full stops (…………..) to represent the missing words.
- Put a number (1-8) before each missing word.
- For each missing word, you need to put a "stem word" at the end of the line. A "stem word" is a word that has to be changed to form the missing word. For example, if the missing word in the text is "surprising," you could use "surprise" as the stem word.

Word formation 3

- In this task, there are a total of eight missing words in the text.
- There is never more than one missing word per line on the page.
- In a word formation task, there is usually at least one answer that is either negative or plural. For example, if the stem word is "possible," the missing word in the text might be "impossible" or "possibilities."

3e Put on your thinking cap(s)*

About the activity

Mediation task type	Leading group work – managing interaction
Mediation strategies	Selecting and omitting information, summarising, explaining
Summary of the activity	Students decide on a solution to a problem together after looking at it from different perspectives, with one of the students taking a leading role.

Rationale

This task not only develops mediation strategies but also leadership skills and the ability to solve problems, both of which have been designated as key 21st Century Skills.

How to run the activity

Levels	B2–C1	Learners	Teens/adults	Time	45–60 minutes

Preparation	- Make a copy of the worksheet for each student. - Choose a problem for your students to discuss. This could be a local or global problem, or even a specific scenario. Note that it helps to make the problem as specific as possible. Here are a few ideas: • Bullying on social media is becoming a big issue. • Your town council is planning to tear up a beloved local park and build a new sports facility. • A friend has stolen something valuable. You promised not to tell anyone, but now an innocent person has been accused of the crime.
Procedure	1. Lead into the activity by asking the students if they are familiar with the English idiom "to put on your thinking cap." Ask them if they have a similar expression in their own language. 2. Explain the activity: students are going to discuss a problem in groups and identify a possible solution. However, they are going to do so following a specific thinking strategy. Together, they will all look at the problem from five different perspectives, i.e. wear five different "thinking caps." Hand out the worksheet and give the students time to read it and ask questions.

* This task is based on a well-known "parallel thinking" activity created by Edward de Bono.

3e Put on your thinking cap(s)

Procedure	3. To further clarify the idea of the hats, select a sample problem, such as "The national government is considering whether or not to ban homework," and elicit or provide statements for what people might say while wearing each of the "thinking caps," i.e. "They don't have homework in Finland, and they have one of the best educational systems in the world (white cap)," or "Without homework, I'd have so much more free time! (red cap)," etc. 4. Make sure that students understand that the idea is NOT that each group member wears a different "thinking cap," but rather that everyone wears the same "thinking cap" at the same time before switching to the next one. Also, check students' understanding of the role of the mediator, who guides the interaction, making sure everyone has the correct "thinking cap" on. The mediator also takes notes on key points or ideas and gives a brief summary of these before everyone in the group switches to a new "thinking cap." 5. Put students into small groups. Nominate one student in each group to be the mediator. 6. Write or project a problem on the board and check the students' understanding. 7. While the students do the activity, circulate and provide support as necessary. Remember to keep the time. Five minutes is generally a good amount of time for each thinking cap. 8. In open class, the mediators from each group take turns explaining what their group decided and how they reached that particular solution. 9. Give feedback on the task.

Language	– Lexis related to the problem (for example, bullying on social media): *parental supervision, spread rumours, be called offensive names*
	– Conditional sentences: *Supposing we limited teenagers access to social media… If we decide to pass a new law, then…*
	– Functional language for:
	  • Intervening to redirect the discussion: *Let's save that thought for later because… Right now we have our green hats on… That's yellow hat thinking…*
	  • Summing up the discussion: *some important points that came up were… everybody liked the idea of…*
	  • Talking about advantages/disadvantages: *Ideally… One upside/downside might be that…*
	  • Discussing feelings/intuitions: *I have the impression that… My instinct is to think that… I don't know exactly why but I think…*

3e Put on your thinking cap(s)

▼▲ Differentiation	- Some students may find looking at a problem from the perspective of one of the "thinking caps" easier than another. This is normal and not a problem for the activity, as long as all the group members participate and contribute equally overall. - If some students are particularly talkative, encourage the mediator to not let them dominate too much and make sure everyone has a chance to share their ideas.
Variation and extension	- Instead of problems, this way of approaching a discussion could be used to talk about a controversial issue/current event, roleplay a meeting, prepare for a group presentation or project, etc. - The order that the students talk about each of the "thinking caps" could be predetermined or the mediator could decide on the fly. One effective order is: white, red, black, yellow, green.
Feedback	Feedback on students in the role of the mediator should focus on how well they were able to: - manage and organise group work - intervene to set group members back on task or redirect the discussion - take effective notes and concisely sum up main points and ideas from the group interaction. Feedback on the participants could focus on how well they are able to: - consistently look at the problem from the given perspective - contribute their ideas and opinions while at the same time not dominating - build on the contributions of their group mates.
Adaptation for the virtual classroom	The open class activities could be done in the main room and the group work in breakout rooms. One student from each group could use the screen sharing function to display the worksheet with the information about the thinking caps, so everyone can easily refer to it during the discussion.

3e Put on your thinking cap(s)

Work in groups. You are going to discuss a problem and decide on a possible solution. During your discussion, all the members of the group will wear the same "thinking cap" at the same time before all switching to the next one. While you are wearing one of the "thinking caps," you should try to only look at the problem from that one perspective.

The white cap looks for facts and information. It is neutral and objective. It is the opposite of the red hat.

The red cap deals with emotions and intuitions. While wearing this hat, think about how something makes you feel, or how it might make other people feel.

The black cap focuses on problems and disadvantages. Note: avoid using the black hat to try to prove other people wrong or attack them.

The yellow cap looks at the positive side of things. It sees advantages and benefits. It is the opposite of the black hat.

The green cap is creative. It looks for new ideas, solutions and alternatives.

The mediator

In each group, one student is the mediator. In this role, you can wear all of the five "thinking caps" and participate in the discussion, but your main job is to manage and organise the discussion. If a student is not looking at the problem from the correct perspective, it is your job to tell them to put on the correct "thinking cap". Also, you need to take notes and provide a brief summary of the key points and ideas from each stage. At the end of the activity, you will explain to the rest of the class what solution your group agreed on and how you decided.

4a (Inter)mediators

4 Mediating communication

4a (Inter)mediators

 About the activity

Mediation task type	Acting as an intermediary in informal situations (with friends and colleagues)
Mediation strategies	Summarising, paraphrasing, translating, explaining sociocultural elements
Summary of the activity	Students do a roleplay in groups of three in which one student takes on the role of an intermediary. The student in this role helps two people who don't share a common language understand each other.

Rationale

This activity gives students useful practice in common, real-world situations involving the use of key mediation strategies.

 How to run the activity

Levels	A2–B2	Learners	Teens/Adults	Time	30 minutes

Preparation	Make enough copies of the worksheet for each group to have a set of role cards. Cut up the cards.
Procedure	1. Lead into the topic by asking students to think of times when they didn't share a common language with somebody and this made it very difficult to communicate. In pairs, ask students to explain where they were and what happened.
	2. Explain the activity: in groups of three, students are going to carry out a roleplay based on a situation where two people can't understand each other's languages and need the help of an intermediary. Each student gets a card with information about their role. Note that if you need to create a group of four, two students can share one of the roles.
	3. Organise the class into groups and distribute the role cards. Check the class's understanding of the fact that students in role A can only use their L1 during the roleplay, while students in role B can only speak English. Students in role C are expected to use their L1 when talking to the student in role A and English when talking to the student in role B.
	4. While the students carry out the roleplay, circulate and provide support if necessary.
	5. Give feedback on the task.

4a (Inter)mediators

Language	- Lexis related to the situation (for example, a clothes shop): *changing room, size, small/medium/large*
	- Reported speech: *He says he needs a bigger size. He is asking if you have this shirt in red.*
	- Functional language for:
	  • Offering to help: *Can I help? Do you need some help translating?*
	  • Apologising: *I'm sorry but I don't speak a word of…, I'm sorry but it's my first time here.*
	  • Making requests: *Can you ask her if…? Can you find out if…?*

▼▲ Differentiation	- The first time you do a roleplay with a class it will be normal for some students to feel inhibited and carry it out somewhat mechanically. In this case, try not to be too critical. The more roleplay activities you bring to class, the more comfortable your students will feel with this type of activity and the more they will get out of it in terms of language and skills development. - Roleplays are a bit different from drama in the sense that they are usually more spontaneous and are not practised and performed for an audience. The emphasis is on the process of playing a part rather than executing a performance. However, if your students are particularly extroverted and enjoy "being on stage," you could invite them to do their roleplays in front of the class.
Variation and extension	Roleplays lend themselves to task repetition, particularly after receiving feedback from the teacher and/or doing a self-reflection stage. For this task, students could either roleplay the same situation again or swap cards and do a different one. In either case, assign a different student the role of the intermediary.
Feedback	This should focus on how well the student in the role of intermediary is able to: - communicate in English the main sense of what is said in their L1 - identify and relay specific information that is particularly important or relevant - give additional explanations if necessary, including the interpretation of sociocultural elements At the end of the roleplay, you could invite students to self-reflect on the task using the following questions: 1. What went particularly well? 2. What could have gone better? 3. How successful was the student in role C in helping the other two people understand each other? 4. Did everyone participate equally? Why or why not? 5. If you were in this same situation in real life, how successful do you think you would be? © DELTA Publishing, 2021 | www.deltapublishing.co.uk ACTIVITIES FOR MEDIATION ISBN 978-3-12-501744-3 by Riccardo Chiappini and Ethan Mansur

4a (Inter)mediators

Adaptation for the virtual classroom	You can set up the roleplays in breakout rooms. You might consider entering the breakout rooms with your video and audio turned off to monitor as unobtrusively as possible. With roleplays, it's best not to intervene unless absolutely necessary. A good option for feedback on student language for this type of activity is taking notes and then later putting these up on the virtual whiteboard, where you can explore a selection of successful and less successful language.

4a (Inter)mediators – the role cards

Situation 1 Role card A	Situation 1 Role card B	Situation 1 Role card C
You're a police officer. Your level of English is very low. You've just seen someone commit a minor infraction, such as throwing rubbish on the ground. You want to give the person a ticket, but when you talk to them, they don't understand you.	You're a tourist. It is your first time in this town or city. Your English is very good, but you don't speak a word of the local language. A police officer comes up and starts talking to you, but you don't understand what they are saying.	You live in this town or city and speak the local language. You have a good level of English. You see a police officer talking to a tourist, but it's obvious they can't understand each other. You offer to help.
Situation 2 Role card A	**Situation 2 Role card B**	**Situation 2 Role card C**
You're a shop assistant. Your level of English is very low. A tourist has just come into your shop and started to ask you questions, but you don't understand what they are saying.	You're a tourist. It's your first time in this town or city. Your English is very good, but you don't speak a word of the local language. You want to buy a special gift to bring back for a family member. You go to a shop and ask the shop assistant about the gift, but they don't understand you.	You live in this town or city and speak the local language. You have a good level of English. You are in a shop and see a tourist trying to explain something to a shop assistant, but it's obvious they can't understand each other. You offer to help.
Situation 3 Role card A	**Situation 3 Role card B**	**Situation 3 Role card C**
You work at a train station. Your level of English is very low. A tourist has just come up to you and started asking you questions, but you don't understand what they are saying.	You're a tourist. It's your first time in this town or city. Your English is very good, but you don't speak a word of the local language. You want to know how to travel to a nearby town to see a well-known tourist attraction. You ask an employee at the train station for information, but they don't understand you.	You live in this town or city and speak the local language. You have a good level of English. You are in a train station and see a tourist trying to explain something to a railway employee, but it's obvious they can't understand each other. You offer to help.

4b Conflicts and disagreements

 About the activity

Mediation task type	Facilitating communication in delicate situations and disagreements
Mediation strategies	Summarising, translating, explaining sociocultural elements
Summary of the activity	Students listen to their partners talk about an argument or situation of conflict they have had with a friend or colleague, and then they suggest a resolution based on what their partners have told them.

Rationale

This task gives students the opportunity to share and reflect on situations of conflict that they might have gone through, as well to give each other ideas on how they could have resolved them.

 How to run the activity

Levels	B1–B2	Learners	Teens/Adults	Time	45 minutes

Preparation	Make a copy of the materials below for each pair of students.
Procedure	1. Lead into the topic by asking students to brainstorm reasons why arguments and conflicts may arise between friends or colleagues (e.g. lack of respect, misunderstandings, missed deadlines, etc.). 2. Explain task: students talk about an argument or situation of conflict they have had with a friend or colleague. (This may have happened at any time in the past). Then students give each other advice on how they could have resolved the conflict. 3. Hand out worksheet. Students do Activity 1 individually and summarise the conflict in a few key points. 4. Organise class into pairs. Assign roles: Students A and Students B. 5. Students A do Activity 2 while Students B do Activity 3: Students A describe the situation of conflict to Students B. Students B take notes and ask Students A further questions to find out more about it. 6. Reverse roles: Students B do Activity 2 and Students A do Activity 3. 7. Allow time for students to prepare to answer question 4 in their worksheet, which asks them to suggest how the conflict could have been resolved. 8. Students A and B do Activity 4: Students B take on the role of mediator and give Students A advice on how the argument or situation of conflict could have been resolved. 9. Reverse roles: Students A act as mediator and give Students B advice on how the argument or situation of conflict has been resolved.

4b Conflicts and disagreements

Procedure	10. In open class, ask students to share some interesting points raised during their conversations with their partners (e.g. a piece of good advice in a particular situation, how bad was a particular argument, etc.). 11. Give feedback on the task.

Language	– Lexis to
	  • talk about conflict: *argue (over), fight (over), shout (at)*
	  • describe negative traits in people: *aggressive, unfriendly, short/bad-tempered, etc.*
	 – Use of present tense to talk about past events: *And then he says that he's not satisfied with the report I've handed in…, She storms in and points her finger at me…*; reporting verbs: *I begged him to stop but…, She was complaining about the fact that…, I'd warned him that this would happen*
	 – Functional language to:
	  • add information and paraphrase: *To put it another way…, What I meant was (that)…*
	  • give opinions: *I reckon…, I'd say…*
	  • ask for advice: *Do you think it's alright to…?, What would you say if I…?*
	  • give advice: *Did you think about…?, One thing you could/should have done is…*

▼▲ Differentiation	Some students may not be happy to talk about a personal conflict or disagreement. In this case, you could ask them to just act as mediators, that is, to listen to their partners, take notes and then recommend a possible solution (Activities 3 and 4 in the worksheet).
Variation and extension	As a follow-up activity, students could choose one of the arguments they have talked about and roleplay it. In this case, make sure that: 1. students brief each other on the important elements to take into account when their partner roleplays the friend or colleague with whom they had the argument (e.g. how they reacted, how they talked, the body language they used, etc.). 2. a third student joins the roleplay acting as mediator: ask them to listen, take notes on the argument and intervene when necessary. At the end, they have to sum up both points of view and help the parties reach a solution.
Feedback	This should focus on how well the students have relayed and understood their partners' situation, as well as how well they have explained the possible resolution to the conflict. 1. *How well have students described the situation/argument? And how well have they explained the different points of view?* 2. *How well have the mediators been able to summarise the situation back to their partner? Were the solutions they proposed appropriate to the situation their partner had described to them?*
Adaptation for the virtual classroom	Switch off your camera and mute your microphone when monitoring in breakout rooms. This will allow students to feel less threatened by your presence when talking about personal negative experiences.

4b Conflicts and disagreements – the worksheet

Activity 1 Think about an argument or situation of conflict you have had with a friend or colleague. This may have happened at any time in the past. Use the table to summarise the situation in a few points.

Where it happened	
What you were doing just before the argument happened	
Who the people involved in the argument were	
Why you argued (consider both your own and your friend's/colleague's point of view)	
Any other details you think are relevant	

Activity 2 Tell your partner about your situation without saying if or how the conflict was resolved. Your partner will take notes and ask you for more information.

Activity 3 Listen to your partner's situation. Take notes and ask them questions to find out more about it. Remember they cannot tell you if and how they resolved the conflict.

Activity 4 Think about the conflict your partner has just described to you. If you were/had been asked to mediate the situation, what would you tell/have told both parties to resolve it? Use the list below to help you.

Suggested steps to take while doing this
1) Look back at your notes and use these to quickly summarise the situation back to your partner.
2) Ask your partner to confirm that what you are saying/have in your notes is correct.
3) Suggest how the conflict could be/have been resolved.
4) Ask your partner what they think of your idea/s.

4c Culture collision

About the activity

Mediation task type	Facilitating pluricultural space
Mediation strategies	Linking to previous knowledge, explaining sociocultural elements
Summary of the activity	Students write a short sketch based on an intercultural encounter and act it out for the class.

Rationale

This task helps develop students' intercultural competence by giving them the opportunity to practise, in the form of a short sketch, creating a "shared space" between people from different cultures.

How to run the activity

Levels	B1–B2	Learners	Adults	Time	45–60 minutes

Preparation	None.
Procedure	1. Lead into the activity by asking students to brainstorm possible sources of cultural misunderstandings in a business context, e.g. how people greet each other, attitudes towards punctuality, hierarchy, etc. You could tell the students a short anecdote during this stage to get them thinking.
	2. Explain the task: students are going to write and perform a short sketch, i.e. a short dramatic performance. The context is a business in the students' country that has been bought by a foreign company. A group of employees from the foreign company have come to oversee the acquisition. Everyone seems to get along well, but certain cultural differences result in misunderstandings. In groups, students create sketches in which these misunderstandings are resolved with the help of one employee who is familiar with both cultures and acts as a mediator.
	3. Put the students into groups of three or four. Assign each group one of the following potential sources of misunderstanding in intercultural encounters: • <u>Communication style:</u> interrupting, remaining silent, being assertive, passive, etc. • <u>Greetings:</u> handshake, kisses, common questions to make small talk, etc. • <u>Eating and food:</u> religious dietary restrictions, eating times, table manners, etc. • <u>National pride:</u> historical figures or events, political systems, sports, etc.
	4. While the students create their sketches, go around and provide support as necessary. Note that students might be tempted to focus on simple stereotypes of other cultures. Encourage them to instead reflect on their own culture and identify customs or behaviours that might be easily misinterpreted by members of a different culture.

4c Culture collision

Procedure	5. The groups take turns acting out their sketch for the rest of the class. Ask the students listening to write down one thing they particularly liked about the sketch. 6. Give feedback on the task.

Language	- Lexis related to the type of misunderstanding (for example, greetings): *Kissing on both cheeks, personal space, social distance*
	- Comparatives: *Here it is much more common for people to… In this situation, we tend to be a bit more formal/informal*
	- Functional language for:
	  • Generalising: *In general, we don't…, As a rule, we shake hands when… Here it's normal to…*
	  • Explaining: *When we say X, it means…, I think what happened was…*

▼▲ Differentiation	Some students might find it difficult to examine their own culture and identify customs or behaviours that people from other cultures might find unusual or unexpected. It would therefore be helpful to think of a couple of ideas for each of the situations on the cards before class, so as to be ready to assist any groups who are having trouble coming up with an idea for a sketch.
Variation and extension	- During the part of the task where students brainstorm ideas, one student could act as the "recorder." Once the group has agreed on an idea and assigned characters, they could adlib the scene a few times (with the recorder taking notes), trying out different ideas. When the group is satisfied with the sketch, the recorder then writes the script with help from the other group members. - The context could be adapted to an international student exchange programme for secondary or university age students. - In multicultural classes, students could maintain their own cultural identities in the sketch.
Feedback	This should focus on how well students are able to create a sketch in which the characters: - Clarify and/or resolve a misunderstanding rooted in cultural differences - Reflect on perspectives and/or worldviews other than their own - During stage 5, students could do the following peer-feedback activity: Watch your classmates perform their sketches. For each sketch, give your classmates a mark from 1–5 (1, not at all, 5 very well) on how well they: • created a realistic situation involving a misunderstanding related to cultural differences • found a way to resolve or explain the misunderstanding • avoided simple stereotypes • reflected on the perspective of people from another culture
Adaptation for the virtual classroom	In breakout rooms, students could write and rehearse their sketches. Using a shared document would allow them to all work on the script together. The sketches could then be performed in the main room. You could use the "spotlight" feature of video conferencing apps like Zoom to make certain users appear more prominently in gallery mode.

4d Debate with moderator

 About the activity

Mediation task type	Facilitating communication in delicate situations and disagreements
Mediation strategies	Selecting and omitting information, summarising
Summary of the activity	After debating a topic, participants must work with a moderator to find common ground.

Rationale

The addition of a moderator to a debate puts a refreshing new twist on a classroom activity that will already be familiar to most language learners. It also develops valuable communication skills that will be helpful for bridging sociocultural gaps or differences in standpoint.

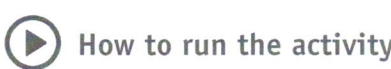 **How to run the activity**

Levels	B2–C1	Learners	Teens/Adults	Time	45–60 minutes

Preparation	Make at least two photocopies of the worksheet and cut up the topic cards.
Procedure	1. Lead into the activity by asking students why it might be a good idea to have a moderator during formal debates, for example, those that take place between political candidates in some countries. 2. Explain the task: Students A and B debate a topic, using the prompts on the cards and their own ideas, while Student C moderates. Stress that A and B must defend the stance on their card – irrelevant of their real opinion. 3. Put students into groups of three. Assign each member of the group one of the following roles: A agrees, B disagrees and C moderates. 4. Each group has a different topic. Give Students A and B their respective cards; Student C gets both cards. Give A and B time to think of reasons and examples to support their arguments. C thinks of possible common ground between the two positions. 5. While A and B debate the topic, C takes notes, intervenes if A or B go off topic and keeps the time (1 or 2 minutes per argument and counter argument). 6. Once the debate is finished, C briefly summarises the main points made by each side and presents a few ideas for possible compromise positions. The students then all work together to find common ground. During this second stage, it's very important for A and B to "come out of their corners" and make a genuine effort to meet in the middle. 7. To round off the activity, ask the groups to share in open class. 8. Give feedback on the task.

4d Debate with moderator

Language	- Expressing agreement/disagreement – *Yes, but…, You make a good point about X, but have you considered …?* - Developing and justifying an argument – *It's common knowledge that…, Many studies show…* - Establishing common ground – *Maybe we can meet half-way, One point of agreement seems to be…* - Lexis related to the topic of debate
▼▲ Differentiation	- Instead of preparing and making arguments on their own, less confident/lower-level students can be paired with more confident/proficient students to form a debate 'team.' - The first time the teacher runs the activity, more confident/higher level students can be assigned the role of mediator.
Variation and extension	This activity lends itself well to task repetition. Students can be given new topic cards and switch roles, with a new student in the role of the mediator. This activity could be personalised by having the students choose their own topics and create their own cards with two or three of their own arguments.
Feedback	This should focus on how well the students in the role of mediators have kept A and B on topic and to the time limits – and, above all, on how well all three students were able to work together to bridge the divide between the two sides during the second stage of the activity.
Adaptation for the virtual classroom	This activity could easily be adapted to synchronous online courses, with students performing the task in breakout rooms and the feedback stage taking place in the main room.

4d Debate with moderator – the topic cards

Topic 1: Agree
Violent video games should be banned.
- Real people are hurt by violence. Is it right to turn this into entertainment?
- There is no way to stop young children from playing video games showing graphic scenes of violence and death.
- Your idea.

Topic 1: Disagree
Violent video games should be banned.
- Studies have shown no link between playing violent video games and real world violence.
- Video games involving warfare and adventure help players develop valuable skills, such as teamwork and problem-solving.
- Your idea.

Topic 2: Agree
All people should have the right to own guns.
- Most gun owners are responsible people who only use their guns for hunting or shooting sports.
- Self-defense is a fundamental human right.
- Your idea.

Topic 2: Disagree
All people should have the right to own guns.
- Police and soldiers are the only people who need to own guns. It's unnecessary and dangerous for regular citizens.
- Guns that are bought legally are often stolen and used by criminals.
- Your idea.

Topic 3: Agree
Homework should not exist.
- Homework takes time away from spending time with family, extracurricular activities, etc.
- Homework is a constant source of conflict between parents and their children.
- Your idea.

Topic 3: Disagree
Homework should not exist.
- Homework teaches students to work independently and develop self-discipline.
- Homework encourages parents to take a more active role in their children's education.
- Your idea.

Topic 4: Agree
Humans should explore and colonise other planets.
- Space exploration expands technology that benefits everybody.
- Humans may be forced to leave earth one day and it's good to have a plan B.
- Your idea.

Topic 4: Disagree
Humans should explore and colonise other planets.
- Space exploration is incredibly expensive. That money could be better spent down here on earth.
- The brilliant people working on space exploration could be helping to solve other more important problems facing humankind.
- Your idea

4e With a little help "for" my friends

 About the activity

Mediation task type	Acting as intermediary in informal situations (with friends and colleagues)
Mediation strategies	Summarising, paraphrasing, translating, adapting language, explaining sociocultural elements
Summary of the activity	Students roleplay different situations in which friends or colleagues talk about familiar activities and experiences but need someone to translate for them to understand each other.

Rationale

In this task, lower level students have the chance to develop key mediation strategies by acting out authentic situations in which they can mediate simple, familiar information (e.g. their hobbies, routines, job).

 How to run the activity

Levels	A1–A2	Learners	Adults	Time	40 minutes

Preparation	– Make a copy of the role cards. Cut up the cards. – Note that each group of three will need a different roleplay situation card. For other set-ups, see Variation and extension section below.
Procedure	1. Lead into the topic by asking students whether they've ever translated for friends or colleagues who didn't understand each other because they didn't speak the same language. Invite students to share their experiences. If your students have never translated for someone or found themselves in similar contexts, ask them to work in pairs and brainstorm informal situations in which friends and/or colleagues might need someone to translate for them. 2. Explain the task: in groups, students roleplay three authentic situations in which people talk about simple, familiar topics but need someone to translate in order for everyone to understand each other. 3. Organise class into groups of three and assign roles: A, B and C. Give students in each group their corresponding role card (A, B or C). If you have groups with more than three students, two of them can share one of the roles. Allow time for students to read their cards and prepare for the roleplay. 4. Students act out their situation. Monitor and assist as necessary. Remind students in Role A that they don't speak English!

4e With a little help "for" my friends

Procedure	5. Once they have finished acting out their situation, assign different roles to the students in each group (e.g. A becomes B, B becomes C and C becomes A). Ask students to pass their role cards to another group (e.g. students in the first group pass their role cards to the second, the second to the third, etc.). Note that this is to make sure that all the students in each group act as mediators (Role C) at least once. The task finishes when all students have acted out all the three situations. 6. In open class, ask students to discuss what they have found easy or difficult (e.g. to translate, explain, etc.), especially when acting in the role of the mediator. 7. Give feedback on the task.

Language	- Lexis related to the situation, e.g. Situation 1: *cousin, free time, memory*
	- Grammar to talk about past events: *I remember when we were younger and…*; present habits, e.g. *I'm taking yoga classes now*;
	- Time expressions: *usually, once, (two years) ago*
	- Functional language to:
	  • show understanding: *I see…, Sure…*
	  • ask for repetition: *Can you repeat, please?, What did he/she say?*
	  • clarify: *He/She said that…, What he/she wants to say is that…*

▼▲ Differentiation	- Some students might not be keen on acting in front of other people. In this case, suggest that they share Role C (mediator) with a partner. - With stronger groups, add an extra challenge by allowing less time to prepare for the roleplay: once you have checked understanding and cleared up any doubts, ask students to start acting it out. This will lead the students to improvise more (by allowing them to think on their feet and make use of the strategies they already have available), which may open up more opportunities to deal with emergent language.
Variation and extension	In the example procedure above, the teacher uses the three roleplay situation cards at the same time. However, if time is an issue, you can have all your groups roleplay one situation at the same time and then either pass on to the other two or save them for other lessons.
Feedback	This should focus on how well the students in the role of the mediator (Role C) have been able to bridge the linguistic, cultural and information gaps between A and B. Here are some questions you could ask yourself when monitoring the roleplay: 1. *Has the mediator passed the information on clearly?* 2. *How well did they convey/translate (e.g. cultural elements, shades of meaning, etc.) from the students' L1 into English?* 3. *When they weren't able to find equivalents in English, which other mediation strategies did they use (e.g. explaining, paraphrasing, summarising, etc.)*
Adaptation for the virtual classroom	Give instructions for the roleplay in the main room. Clear any doubts students might have before sending them into their breakout rooms, but remind them that you will be joining each room to monitor and support them as necessary.

4e With a little help "for" my friends – the situation cards

Situation 1: Long lost relatives — Role A	Situation 1: Long lost relatives — Role B	Situation 1: Long lost relatives — Role C
Your American relative has come to visit you for the first time. You have never met them before and you don't speak English. You asked a friend to translate for you and your relative. The three of you are together now. You want to tell your American relative a bit about yourself (who you are, your friends and family, your hobbies, etc.) and ask them some questions to find out more about them.	You are American and are visiting a relative in a foreign country. It's the first time that you meet them. Your relative doesn't speak English and has asked a friend to translate for you and your relative. The three of you are together now. You want to tell your relative a bit about yourself (who you are, your friends and family, your hobbies, etc.) and ask them some questions to find out more about him/her.	Your friend is with an American relative. They don't speak English and his/her relative doesn't speak your language. You speak English so your friend asked you to help them understand each other. Translate for them.

Situation 2: Meeting with landlord — Role A	Situation 2: Meeting with landlord — Role B	Situation 2: Meeting with landlord — Role C
You are looking for a flat to rent in London. You have found one you like and now you are going to meet the landlord/lady. The landlord doesn't live in the flat, but they want to know more about you. You don't speak English, but you have a friend who is going to translate for you and the landlord/lady. Tell the landlord/lady a bit about yourself (what you do, your daily routine, etc.) and ask them some questions about the flat.	You have a flat in London and want to rent it out. One person is coming to see the flat today. You don't live in the flat, but you want to know if this person is a good tenant. Ask them some questions to know more about the person and give them some information about the flat (how much it is, if there are any special rules the tenant should respect, etc.)	You are helping a friend from your country who wants to rent a flat in London. They don't speak English but you do. Today your friend is going to meet the landlord/lady of a flat they like. You are going to the meeting to help them understand each other. Translate for them.

Situation 3: Break at international job fair — Role A	Situation 3: Break at international job fair — Role B	Situation 3: Break at international job fair — Role C
You are at an international job fair with a colleague. During the break your colleague meets a friend from Ireland. Your colleague's friend asks you about your job. You don't speak English, but your colleague does so he/she is going to translate for you. Tell your colleague's friend about your job (what you do, what you like, what you find easy or difficult, etc.) and then ask them to do the same.	You are Irish. You are at an international job fair. During the break you meet a friend. Your friend is with someone who is from your friend's country and doesn't speak English. Ask them about their job (what they do, what they like, what they find easy or difficult in their job etc.) and then tell them about your job (what you do, what you like, what you find easy or difficult, etc.).	You are at an international job fair with a colleague. During the break you meet a friend from Ireland. They start talking but your colleague doesn't speak English. Translate for them.

4f Host family meeting

 About the activity

Mediation task type	Facilitating pluricultural space
Mediation strategies	Summarising, combining, explaining sociocultural elements
Summary of the activity	Students roleplay a situation in which they discuss different eating habits and come to an agreement.

Rationale

This task helps lower-level students develop useful mediation strategies and sociocultural awareness by discussing simple information such as food and meal times in different countries.

 How to run the activity

Levels	A2–B1
Learners	Teens
Time	45 minutes

Preparation	– Make a copy of the role cards for each group of four students. Cut up the cards. – Note that if you have a group of three, you can leave out either role card B, C or D (role card A is for the mediator).
Procedure	1. Ask students if they've ever lived with a host family in a foreign country. Invite them to share their experiences to elicit the different eating habits their host family/culture had and how different they were from their own. In case students have never had this experience, ask them to work in pairs and brainstorm different eating habits in their culture and Britain. 2. Explain task: students roleplay a situation in which three foreign students have just arrived at their host family's house in England. The students are going to live there for two weeks while studying English at a summer school nearby. One student will take the role of the host mother/father, who will be leading a discussion for the guests to agree on what they will have for breakfast/lunch/dinner, as well as what time they will have each meal during their stay in the house. As they do this, they'll have to write up a weekly menu showing the meals they have agreed on. Note that in the example menu in the materials section below, the days of the week are shown in groups of two/three. This is for students to come up with ideally one or a maximum of two dishes/types of food per group of days (e.g. on Monday, Thursday and Sundays they'll have *pasta* OR *either pasta or chicken and roast potatoes*, etc.).

4f Host family meeting

Procedure	3. Organise the class into groups of four and assign roles (A, B, C and D). Give students in each group their corresponding role card (A, B, C or D). If you have three students in one group, leave out one of the foreign students' role cards. 4. Allow time for students to read their cards and ask you questions. Once they have all understood what to do, ask them to choose a name for their character and prepare for their roleplay. 5. Students act out the roleplay. Monitor and assist as necessary. Remind B, C and D that they should obviously defend their customs, but since they have to come to an agreement (write up the menu), they will also have to be open to compromise. Also, remind students in the role of the host mother/father that they shouldn't make decisions for their guests themselves, but rather help them towards an agreement. 6. In open class, ask students to share and comment on the activity (e.g. what they found easy/challenging). 7. Give feedback on the task.

Language	– Lexis to describe the different food preferences of each foreign student: *liver pâté, oatmeal, stew*
	– Time expressions: *early, late, after*
	– Sequencers: *first, afterwards, at the end*
	– Functional language to:
	  • suggest and recommend: *Maybe we can have cereal and milk instead? You all like roast potatoes so we could…*
	  • ask for repetition: *Can you repeat, please?, What is it that you (like/don't like)?*
	  • reformulate ideas and opinions of others: *Like he said…, We all said that…*
	  • summarise key points agreed on during the conversation: *All of us agree that…, So everyone would like to have…*

▼▲ **Differentiation**	– Some students might have problems understanding/describing some of the foods mentioned in their role cards. After handing these out (stage 3), ask your students to look up the words they don't understand in the dictionary (or on the internet using their phones) in pairs or small groups and then to report back to class. – With stronger groups, raise the challenge by asking students to produce a more detailed menu (e.g. with desserts options, drinks, Sunday or weekend specials, etc.).

4f Host family meeting

Variation and extension	With multilingual classes, ask Students B, C and D to create their own role cards in which they can include their eating habits and preferences (since each family/individual will have different habits, do encourage them to include information that is generally true for people from their country/culture!). In this case, Student A (host mother/father or mediator) will have to take a photo of the three new cards the other students will have produced and refer to this when reading the first column in their role card.
Feedback	This should focus on 1) how well the students in the role of guests (B, C and D) have mediated the information from their cards into the conversation/interaction with the other students, and 2) how well the students in the role of host mother/father have mediated between the different points of view. Some questions you might want to answer while monitoring might be: ***Guests*** 1. How well have they used the information on their cards to explain their position/views? 2. Did they include all the points that were relevant for the conversation? Did they explain them appropriately? 3. How well have they negotiated their views with those of the other guests? Have they tried to find middle ground when necessary? ***Host mother/father*** 1. How well have they managed the conversation between their guests? 2. Have they supported their guests by helping them respect each other's views? 3. At the same time, have they suggested ways for their guests to overcome any disagreement?
Adaptation for the virtual classroom	Rewrite the cards on an online document so that you can easily share them with each of your students.

4f Host family meetings – the role cards

Role A (mediator)			
Instructions for mediator	**Role B**	**Role C**	**Role D**
Read the information about each of your guests (B, C and D) and prepare to help them agree on what they would like to have for breakfast, lunch and dinner during their stay in your house. Together, you and your guests will have to create a weekly menu that makes everyone feel at home.	1) Name:	1) Name:	1) Name: ....
	2) From: Italy	2) From: Norway	2) From: Spain
	3) Breakfast YOU WANT: biscuits, cereal or croissant and milk; WHEN: between 7 and 8am YOU DON'T WANT: savoury food; to have breakfast after 8am!	3) Breakfast YOU WANT: bread, crackers or toast with raw vegetables and liver pâté, and milk WHEN: between 7 and 8am YOU DON'T WANT: sweet food, to have breakfast after 8am!	3) Breakfast YOU WANT: biscuits or cereal and milk, sometimes toast with tomato and orange juice WHEN: between 8 and 9am YOU DON'T WANT: to have breakfast before 8am!
	4) Lunch YOU WANT: pasta, soup, stew WHEN: between 1 and 2pm YOU DON'T WANT: to eat after 2pm!	4) Lunch YOU WANT: sandwich, soup, stew WHEN: between 12 and 1pm YOU DON'T WANT: to eat after 1pm!	4) Lunch YOU WANT: lentils, omelette, sandwiches WHEN: between 2 and 3pm YOU DON'T WANT: soup, stew, to eat before 2pm!
	5) Dinner YOU WANT: chicken, meat, roast potatoes, vegetables, water/fizzy drinks WHEN: between 7:30 and 8pm YOU DON'T WANT: fish, to have dinner after 8pm!	5) Dinner YOU WANT: chicken, fish, roast potatoes, vegetables, water/fizzy drinks WHEN: between 5 and 7pm YOU DON'T WANT: red meat, to have dinner after 7pm – but you like a snack	5) Dinner YOU WANT: chicken, red meat, roast potatoes, water/fizzy drinks WHEN: between 9 and 10pm YOU DON'T WANT: fish, to have dinner before 9pm!

4f Host family meetings – the role cards

Role B	Role C	Role D
You are one of the guest students. Use the information below to introduce yourself and talk about 1) what you'd like to have for breakfast, lunch and dinner. 2) what time you'd like to have these meals.	*You are one of the guest students. Use the information below to introduce yourself and talk about 1) what you'd like to have for breakfast, lunch and dinner. 2) what time you'd like to have these meals.*	*You are one of the guest students. Use the information below to introduce yourself and talk about 1) what you'd like to have for breakfast, lunch and dinner. 2) what time you'd like to have these meals.*
1) Name:	1) Name:	1) Name:
2) From: Italy	2) From: Norway	2) From: Spain
3) Breakfast YOU WANT: biscuits, cereal or croissant and milk; WHEN: between 7 and 8am YOU DON'T WANT: savoury food; to have breakfast after 8am!	3) Breakfast YOU WANT: bread, crackers or toast with raw vegetables and liver pâté, and milk WHEN: between 7 and 8am YOU DON'T WANT: sweet food, to have breakfast after 8am!	3) Breakfast YOU WANT: biscuits or cereal and milk, sometimes toast with tomato and orange juice WHEN: between 8 and 9am YOU DON'T WANT: to have breakfast before 8am!
4) Lunch YOU WANT: pasta, soup, stew WHEN: between 1 and 2pm YOU DON'T WANT: to eat after 2pm!	4) Lunch YOU WANT: sandwich, soup, stew WHEN: between 12 and 1pm YOU DON'T WANT: to eat after 1pm!	4) Lunch YOU WANT: lentils, omelette, sandwiches WHEN: between 2 and 3pm YOU DON'T WANT: soup, stew, to eat before 2pm!
5) Dinner YOU WANT: chicken, meat, roast potatoes, vegetables, water/fizzy drinks WHEN: between 7:30 and 8pm YOU DON'T WANT: fish, to have dinner after 8pm!	5) Dinner YOU WANT: chicken, fish, roast potatoes, vegetables, water/fizzy drinks WHEN: between 5 and 7pm YOU DON'T WANT: red meat, to have dinner after 7pm – but you like a snack like oatmeal after 7pm!	5) Dinner YOU WANT: chicken, red meat, roast potatoes, vegetables, water/fizzy drinks WHEN: between 9 and 10pm YOU DON'T WANT: fish, to have dinner before 9pm!

Menu	What time?	Mon./Thu./Sun.	Tue./Fri.	Wed./Sat.
Breakfast				
Lunch				
Dinner				

5 How to create tasks and adapt materials

If the materials you are working with don't include mediation tasks, or you feel your students need more practice, you may want to create your own tasks and/or adapt the materials you are working with. In this chapter, we outline the main ingredients of a mediation task and a suggested procedure to help you create an effective one.

1. The specific group of learners we are creating the task for

On top of taking into consideration their age, level and needs, we should also think about the different contexts in which our group of students will be more likely to mediate information both inside and outside the formal context of the language classroom. In Appendix 5 of the CEFRCV (2020, p. 198), we can find examples of situations categorised according to the type of mediation and to the four different domains of language use typically dealt with at each different proficiency level: personal, public, occupational and educational. For example, Business English students will generally mediate in the occupational domain, EAP students will be more likely to mediate in public and educational contexts, secondary students, on the other hand, in the personal and educational.

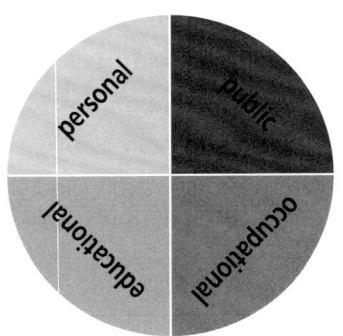

2. The CEFRCV

The next step is to select a) the type of mediation we want our students to practise, and b) the specific descriptor (or descriptors) around which we want to build our task.

a) Type of mediation
In the CEFRCV (2020:90), the three types of mediation are defined as follows:
- passing on new information in an appropriate form (Mediating a text)
- collaborating to construct new meaning (Mediating concepts)
- creating the space and conditions for communicating (Mediating communication)

The type of mediation we select will therefore also define the type of interaction, as illustrated below:

 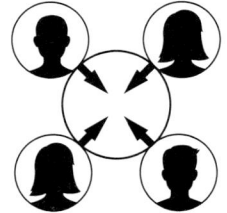 

Mediating a text **Mediating concepts** **Mediating communication**

5 How to create tasks and adapt materials

b) The descriptor

A single descriptor can give us enough information to plan a whole task. Here is an example descriptor for Relaying specific information in speech from the Mediating a text macro group at B2 level:

> **B2** *Can relay in a written report relevant decisions that were taken in a meeting* (Council of Europe 2020, p. 94)

This descriptor already tells us:

1. what we can expect our students to be able to do at a given level
2. the type of texts our students will be able to manipulate (written report)
3. the type of contexts within which we can base the task we want to create (meeting)

3. Situations in which mediation is required

Once we have selected the descriptor, we need to build a situation around it where mediation is necessary. To do this, we would need to define:

a. The reasons why mediation is necessary
b. Who the mediator (or group of mediators) is
c. Who the target audience is
d. The purpose of the target text

Using the descriptor above, we can start thinking about a possible situation:

a. An important meeting and the meeting minutes need to be passed on to the board of directors. None of the directors can attend the meeting.
b. An employee who has attended the meeting
c. The board of directors who couldn't attend the meeting
d. To inform the board of directors of what has been discussed during the meeting

In the example descriptor above, we already have information as per the type of target text our students will have to produce (written report), and the content of the source information they will have to relay through their report (relevant decisions taken in a meeting). Using the situation outlined in a-d above, the source text could be an audio recording of the meeting, but also the written notes from the meeting (minutes), from which the mediator will select only the relevant points and explain them in their report.

4. Mediation strategies and other competences

Once we have built an appropriate situation around the descriptor we have selected, we will be better prepared to predict which strategies, knowledge and other competences our students will have to possess and use to carry out the task successfully (Chiappini, 2021).

Continuing with the same example situation, if we select an audio recording of a meeting as source text, then one of the strategies our students will have to use will be summarising/streamlining information. One example descriptor taken from the CEFRCV for this strategy could then be the following:

> **B2** Can simplify a source text by excluding non-relevant or repetitive information and taking into consideration the intended audience
> (Council of Europe, 2020, p. 122)

175

5 How to create tasks and adapt materials

However, if we opt to find or create some written notes (e.g. the sketched minutes of the meeting) and use these as source text instead, then our students will also be explaining, exemplifying and expanding on the main points from the notes:

| B2 | Can make the content of a text on a subject in their fields of interest more accessible to a target audience by adding examples, reasoning and explanatory comments (Council of Europe, 2020, p. 122) |

As well as making sure that our students possess prior knowledge of the topic that the task requires, we should also make a list of the lexical items and structures that they will need to understand and use to complete it. In this example task, for instance, our students need to be familiar with the topic of the meeting, relevant technical, business-related vocabulary, as well as useful language that will enable them to tackle the source text and create their target text. In order to make sure students have the key language they need to complete the task, we can either pre-teach it before the task or at some point during the task cycle (e.g. before they start producing their target text).

To complete the task successfully, that is, to be able to tackle the source text and produce the target text, on top of mediation strategies and language, we will also have to make sure that our students possess other relevant competences. For example, they will need to know how to organise information and which register to use in a written report (pragmatic competence) and will need to understand and be able to explain socio cultural elements in a text (pluricultural competence). For more information on these competences, refer to Chapter 1.

5. Rubric and worksheet

Now that we have all the ingredients laid out on our desk, it is time for us to put them together. Following the example situation above, the rubric could be:

> Your company has recently merged with a foreign company. You and other managers have met earlier today to discuss the points on the agenda and have produced the minutes below. The new board of directors could not attend the meeting. Write a report for the board to inform them of what was discussed in the meeting.

As a worksheet then, the students could receive the written minutes of the meeting, which our students will need to explain and expand on in their report to the board of directors.

Considerations for adapting materials

All we have said about creating mediation tasks so far is also true for adapting pre-existing materials. When adapting our resources, however, we also have to take the following into consideration:

- **Mediating a text:** All the texts in our coursebooks, whether they be written, spoken or visual, could potentially be turned into source texts. Once we have selected an appropriate text from the unit of work we are covering, we need to identify what will be an appropriate situation in which the source text can work, that is, to whom it can be mediated (target audience) and through what type of text it can be mediated (target text).

- **Mediating concepts:** To give group work more of a "mediation" flavour, we could give each student in a group different roles and responsibilities. For example, if they collaborate in project work to create a poster on a given topic, we could task one student with taking care of deciding what to write in the texts that will go on the poster, another student with finding or drawing appropriate pictures, and another one with taking notes to summarise the progress the whole group's making.

- **Mediating communication:** At the centre of all mediation activities is the mediator, and even more so in mediating communication activities. We can create roleplay situations around the most common topics we can find in coursebooks for our students to moderate a debate (climate change policies, difficult relationships and violence in sports), bridge knowledge and culture gaps (popular beliefs, body language and celebrations) between two or more people. One way to do this is by adding in the role of the mediator who will lead the discussion to resolve conflicts, and offer space for pluriculturalism and understanding.

Further tips

1. Sometimes one descriptor may be sufficient for us to create a whole task. Others, though, we might want to use more than one descriptor, for example to make sure that we include a focus on other types of activities that our students will have to perform within the task, such as Note-taking, Relaying specific information, Translating, etc.
2. Depending on the type of source text or target text we want our students to produce, we can obviously make tweaks to the descriptor/s we have selected. For example, if the descriptor mentions that learners can produce a written report to relay information from a meeting, we could turn the report into an oral presentation to the company's stakeholders or even into a text message to a peer (a colleague) if we want to make it easier, more difficult or simply more motivating.
3. Texts, topics and situations that aren't directly related to the unit of work we are covering, can still engage our students personally and cognitively. However, these shouldn't only be based on real-life contexts either. Some of them might indeed be inappropriate in some teaching and learning contexts. In this case, less realistic and inauthentic scenarios may in fact be more adequate.

Creating cross-linguistic mediation tasks

As we have seen in the first chapter, in cross-linguistic mediation tasks the source texts we can use for Mediating a text activities will have to be in the students' L1. For the same reason, the roleplays we can use for Mediating concepts and Mediating communication activities will have to include one or more roles of people who don't understand English and need someone to mediate (in this case, translate) for them.

If we want to create this type of mediation task, then, we should ask ourselves: *Are we teaching a monolingual or multilingual group of students? How proficient are we in our students' first language or languages?*

If we are teaching a monolingual group, being proficient in our students' L1 will come in handy at the time of finding or writing up the source text in our students' L1 when creating cross-linguistic tasks for Mediating a text activities. Teaching students who share the same L1 will also make it easier for us to create concepts and communication tasks, because the students engaged in roleplay for collaborating in a group (concepts), or mediating between parties (communication), will certainly share the first language with at least one of their group members or with one of the parties. Moreover, if we are proficient in our students' L1, we will also be more prepared to assess our students' mediation performance since we will be better

5 How to create tasks and adapt materials

able to check "which" information has been relayed from the L1 to English as well as "how" they have relayed it.

If we aren't proficient in our students L1, however, there are still a few tricks we could use to bypass the main "linguistic hurdle" to run Mediating a text tasks, both at the teaching and the assessment level. For example, we could use source texts that have been translated professionally (brochures from the local tourism office, films in your students' L1 with subtitles available in English, etc.) and use the translation to monitor as well as give feedback on the task (Chiappini & Mansur, 2020).

When it comes to teaching multilingual classes, though, things get even more complicated. To begin with, we might not speak all our students' first languages. Therefore, we won't be able to find or write up appropriate texts – or as many texts as necessary – for a Mediating a text task. A good trick here would be to ask our students to find the source text themselves. For example, we could ask them to imagine that a friend has come to visit them in their country and has lost something valuable while using public transport. Each of our students can then find information in their own L1 on the website of an official public transport company in their city or country, and then relay it in English to their friend to say what they have to do. The same is true for Mediating communication tasks since we might not be able to have two students speaking the same language in the same group and in all the groups we can form.

Last but not least, if we don't speak our students' first language and have no cheat sheet or professional translation to rely on, it will only be possible to give feedback on some mediation strategies and aspects of overall task achievement, but obviously not others. For example, we won't be able to judge how well our students have selected or omitted information from the source text in their L1, but we might still be able to judge whether the information included in the target text is relevant to the target audience. As we will see in the next chapter, in fact, to assess how well our students mediate texts, we ideally need to assess more than just what they produce.

6 Assessing mediation

1 Introduction

As we have seen in the introduction, mediation involves both reception and production, and frequently also interaction. In a typical Mediating a text task, for example, students read or listen to a source text (reception) and then reformulate and relay the key information to a new target audience either in speech or in writing (production/interaction). In mediating concepts and communication tasks, on the other hand, students listen (reception), speak (production) and react to and build on each other's contributions (interaction). In order to assess mediation tasks it is therefore important to take into account and evaluate each of these modes of language activity.

A further twist is added by the fact that there are also a variety of strategies to consider when students are involved in mediation, such as selecting and omitting information, paraphrasing, breaking down complicated information, etc. (see Chapter 1). Any successful mediation involves the successful use of these strategies. Without them, mediation is not possible. For that reason, the use of mediation strategies appropriate to the task deserves an important place in any assessment of mediation. Focusing on mediation strategies also has an interesting advantage: a number of these strategies, such as summarising, paraphrasing and explaining, involve both reception and production, so by assessing these you are assessing both receptive and productive aspects of the task *at the same time*.

The presence of all these modes and strategies indeed makes assessing mediation tasks a challenging process, or at least more challenging than closed-ended tasks that focus only on reception or production. So how should we go about assessing all these elements of a mediation task?

2 How to give feedback

Research has shown that feedback is an effective tool to promote learning (Boyd et al, 2019). In our experience, this is no less true for mediation, which is why we feel it is an essential stage in any mediation task cycle. This feedback could take various forms: you, the teacher, could be the one giving the feedback and/or your students could be doing peer feedback or self-evaluation activities.

Teacher-led feedback

A lesson stage at the end of an activity where you review aims and consolidate the students' learning, often referred to as a "plenary," is a natural way to round off many mediation activities, because it brings the class back together after group or pair work and adds a sense of closure. It is also a particularly appropriate moment for feedback. The focus of the feedback you give will of course be quite different depending on the type of mediation activity the students have carried out. However, while you are monitoring and giving feedback on a mediation task, our advice is to focus your attention primarily on task achievement and the use of mediation strategies. As we have seen, the primary aim of a mediation activity is to mediate. Therefore, the primary focus of feedback on a mediation task should be how well students were able to complete the task—that is, to 'do' mediation. The more specifically your feedback is focused on the "mediation" aspects of the task, the more effective it will be at helping students perform better as mediators in the future. For this reason, in the teacher's notes, we have also included feedback suggestions for each task. These often take the form of a list of questions to consider, such as those from **2.2a Gaming Galore**, where students must produce an essay that includes information from an infographic:

6 Assessing mediation

- Have they used relevant points from the infographic to answer the essay question?
- How well have they explained these?
- How well have they combined their opinion and their selection of data from the infographic?
- How relevant are the examples provided to support their opinion?
- Is the style appropriate?

Self-evaluation and peer feedback

However, we feel that assessing learning and performance should not only be the teacher's job. One interesting alternative to teacher-led feedback is to give students the opportunity to evaluate themselves and/or their classmates. Note that in this book we use the terms "self-evaluation" and "peer feedback" to include not only activities focused on reflection and evaluating performance or learning, but also activities where students award marks. In general, this type of learner-centred assessment is valuable because it can help students become more autonomous and independent learners, developing metacognitive learning strategies to monitor and improve their own performance without the help of the teacher (Oxford, 2011).

In this book, you will have noticed that this type of self-evaluation or peer-feedback activity can take a number of different forms. For example, students could award themselves marks, as in this self-evaluation task from **3e DIY word formation**, where students work in groups to create an exam task:

… students mark themselves from 1–5 (1 needs work, 2 satisfactory, 3 good, 4 very good, 5 excellent) on the following aspects of group work:

How well did I …
- participate?
- contribute ideas?
- help keep the group on task?
- complete my fair share of the work?
- fulfil my specific responsibilities?

Or they could award marks to other students, as in this example from **4c Culture collision**, where students write and perform sketches based on an intercultural encounter:

… for each sketch, give your classmates a mark from 1–5 (1, not at all, 5 very well) on how well they:
- created a realistic situation involving a misunderstanding related to cultural differences
- found a way to resolve or explain the misunderstanding
- avoided simple stereotypes
- reflected on the perspective of people from another culture

Or students could simply discuss a few questions in pairs, as in this example from **2.4e Signs and notices**:

… students could discuss the following questions (in English or their L1):
- How clear and easy to understand were your partner's translations?
- What strategies did you use when you didn't know a specific word? How successful were you?
- Do you think you could do this type of translation activity in real life? Why or why not?

We have also included photocopiable self-evaluation and peer-feedback activities, such as those in **2.1f Nail your essay!**, **2.2c Elections** and **2.3c Tips for new parents**, among others. In our experience, we have found that self-evaluation and peer-feedback activities lend themselves well to mediation tasks, and we would encourage teachers to experiment with these while running mediation activities. For a wider variety of this type of activity, and a more in-depth look at assessment in the ELT classroom, we suggest consulting *Activities for Alternative Assessment* (2021) by Leo Selivan, a recent addition to DELTA Publishing's "Ideas in Action" series.

6 Assessing mediation

If you are inspired to create your own mediation activities, as we hope you are, and you would like to design a peer-feedback or self-evaluation task to accompany it, the first step is to establish specific, achievable success criteria for the activity. Once again, the 'can do" descriptors in the CEFRCV are an invaluable resource for setting aims. If you have a clear idea of what your students could be expected to do at their level, it not only helps you design a task that provides the appropriate level of challenge, as we have seen in the **How to create tasks and adapt materials** section, but it can also help you develop success criteria that your students can use to assess their own or their classmates' performance. One idea is to show the class a simplified version of a "can do" descriptor you used to create the activity at the beginning of the lesson to establish the learning aim, and then revisit this aim at the end of the task during a peer or self-assessment activity. Naturally, if the aim of the mediation activity is clear from the beginning, it will make it easier for students to determine how successful they were in reaching it.

Rubrics

Another way to assess mediation activities, which can potentially combine both teacher-led feedback and self-evaluation or peer feedback, is to use rubrics. Here is an example of how a self-evaluation activity, like the one from **3e DIY word formation**, can be adapted into a rubric.

Rating:

1. needs work
2. satisfactory
3. good
4. very good
5. excellent

	How well did I…?	You	Teacher
A	participate?		
B	contribute ideas?		
C	help keep the group on task?		
D	complete my fair share of the work?		
E	fulfil my specific responsibilities?		

When creating a rubric, you should try to make the success criteria you have selected as easy-to-read and student-friendly as possible. When students have the chance to first evaluate their own performance and/or their classmates', and then compare their evaluations with the teacher's, they will be better able to see their own strengths and weaknesses, as well as gather invaluable information to understand which specific areas they will have to focus on the next time they do a mediation task. This is also a great way for students to develop competences associated with "learning how to learn", thus helping them take charge of their own progression.

As we have seen, mediation tasks can be quite complex, involving a combination of a variety of modes and strategies. In addition, one mediation task can look completely different to another one, as you will have seen from the wide variety of activities in this book that can be included under the umbrella of mediation. For this reason, we suggest that a one-size-fits-all approach to assessing meditation is not likely to be effective. It can be rather difficult indeed to write a single set of questions, or create a single rubric, self-evaluation or peer-feedback activity that would work for all mediation tasks. Instead, we would encourage you to take the approach we have taken in this book, which is to first identify success criteria for each

6 Assessing mediation

separate task you plan to use, and then consider how best to assess that specific criteria, whether it be through teacher-led or more student-centred assessment activities, or some combination of both.

Here are a few final tips for assessing the three types of mediation defined in the CEFRCV:

- Since the aim of a **mediating a text** task is for the student/mediator to help someone else understand the contents of a written, spoken or visual text, in order to assess this type of mediation it is crucial to evaluate whether and how well the information or message has in fact been communicated.
- One of the main aims of a **mediating concepts** task, on the other hand, is for students/team members to collaborate to produce a final product (e.g. a presentation, poster or a solution to a problem). This means that the main focus of our evaluation should be on the process the students/team members have gone through to create the final product as well as the final product itself.
- Finally, for **mediating communication** tasks, the most important thing to evaluate is whether and how the parties involved in the mediation process have understood each other or found common ground.

Pitfalls

There are a couple of important pitfalls to avoid when assessing mediation. The first is to focus too much on production. It's easy to simply assess a students' performance on a mediation task the way we would a regular speaking or writing task, evaluating their lexical/grammatical range, discourse management/organisation, etc. This is the part of their performance we can most easily observe. However, this ignores all the important work students have to do during the receptive part of the task, as well as the variety of the strategies they need to use in order to, for example, successfully reformulate and pass information from a source to target text.

The second is to focus too much on language control. As we have seen, the main aim of any mediation task is for the students to call upon all of their competences – linguistic, sociolinguistic, pragmatic and so on – to successfully facilitate understanding or interaction. If they achieve this communicative aim, they have successfully "done" mediation. We believe that too much importance placed on language control could create negative washback by pushing students to double down on improving their grammar and vocabulary, rather than encouraging them to improve their ability to use the group of strategies and competences that come under the umbrella term of mediation.

Mediation in exams

As mentioned in the "History of Mediation" section in Chapter 1, mediation began to be included by name in official exams in Europe after the publication of the CEFR 2001. This has only accelerated with the release of the CEFRCV, which provides examination boards with specific descriptors to assess students' performance. In official exams across Europe, from Spain to Austria, it is now common to find "spoken mediation" tasks, where students have to discuss the contents of a source text in a monologue or a spoken interaction, or "written mediation" tasks, where students have to do so in writing.

As you will have seen, *Activities for Mediation* focuses primarily on the ELT classroom. We are mainly concerned with how to create and use mediation tasks in class and how to help students improve their ability to perform such tasks. An in-depth discussion of how mediation can and should be assessed in official exams is, therefore, beyond the scope of this book. It is worth noting, however, that the assessment of mediation is a much discussed topic in the field of language testing at the moment, with presentations on this topic regularly included in the conferences of EALTA (European Association for Language Testing and Assessment) and ALTE (Association of Language Testers in Europe), among others. It will be interesting to watch this discussion continue and see what kind of consensus emerges about the best way to assess mediation in a valid and reliable way in official exams.

References

Anderson, J. (2018). Reimagining English language learners from a translingual perspective. *ELT Journal, 72*(1), 26-37. https://doi.org/10.1093/elt/ccx029

Anderson, J. (2019). *Activities for cooperative learning: making groupwork and pairwork effective in the ELT classroom.* Stuttgart: DELTA Publishing.

Boyd E., Green A., Hopfenbeck TN., Stobart G. (2019). Effective feedback: the key to successful assessment for learning, ELT position papers: Oxford University Press.

Bygate, M. (2009). Effects of task repetition on the structure and control of oral language, In Van den Branden, K., Bygate, M., Norris, J. (eds.) *Task-based language teaching: A reader*, John Benjamins, Amsterdam.

Chiappini, R. (2020). Placing the learner in the leading role, *Advancing Learning blog*, Macmillan, 19 November.
Retrieved from: https://www.macmillanenglish.com/us/blog-resources/articles/article/advancing-learning-placing-the-learner-in-the-leading-role

Chiappini, R. (2020). Mediation tasks for young learners, *Advancing Learning blog*, Macmillan, 19 August.
Retrieved from: https://www.macmillanenglish.com/us/blog-resources/articles/article/advancing-learning-mediation-tasks-for-young-learners.

Chiappini, R. (2021). Skilful language use in writing, *English Teaching professional* 132, p16–18, Pavilion.

Chiappini, R. & Mansur, E. (2020). Cross-linguistic mediation, *English Teaching Professional*, issue 126.

Chiappini, R. & Mansur, E. (2020). Mediating communication: the role of roleplay, *English Teaching Professional*, issue 127.

Chiappini, R. & Mansur, E. (2020). *Oxford mediation course*, Oxford University Press España.
Retrieved from: http://oxfordprogramasdeformacion.com/cursosonline/curso-mediacion-oxford/.

Cook, G. (2010). *Translation in language teaching.* Oxford: Oxford University Press.

Coste, D. & Cavalli, M. (2015). *Education, mobility, otherness: The mediation functions of schools.* Strasbourg: Council of Europe DGII – Directorate General of Democracy.

Council of Europe (2001). *Common European framework of reference for languages: learning, teaching, assessment*, Cambridge: Press Syndicate of the University of Cambridge.

Council of Europe (2020). *Common European framework of reference for languages: learning, testing, assessment: Companion volume.* Council of Europe Publishing, Strasbourg.

Deller S. & Rinvolucri, M. (2002) *Using the mother tongue*, Peaslake: DELTA Publishing.

Dendrinos, B. (2006). Mediation in communication, language teaching and testing. *Journal of Applied Linguistics*, 22: 9–35.

Dendrinos, B. (2013). Testing and teaching mediation. *Directions in English Language Teaching and Testing 1*. Athens: RCEL Publishing.

Figueras, N. (2012). The impact of the CEFR, *ELT Journal*, 66(4): 477–485.

Goodier, T. (2020). Advancing learning: classroom opportunities for mediation, *Advancing learning blog*. Macmillan 15 September.
Retrieved from: https://www.macmillanenglish.com/es/blog-resources/article/al.

References

Goodier, T. (2020). *Mediation and young learners*, Pearson Experiences, Pearson. Retrieved from: https://www.youtube.com/watch?v=ndDp2ekEgTA.

Lantolf, J. (2000). *Sociocultural theory and second language learning*, Oxford: Oxford University Press.

May, S. (2013). *The multilingual turn: Implications for SLA, TESOL, and bilingual education*. Routledge.

Oxford, R. (2011). *Teaching and researching language learning strategies*. Harlow: Pearson Education Limited.

Piccardo, E. & North, B. (2019). *The action-oriented approach*. Bristol: Multilingual matters.

Piccardo, E., North, B & Goodier, T. (2019). Broadening the scope of language education: mediation, plurilingualism, and collaborative learning: the CEFR companion volume, *Journal of e-Learning and Knowledge Society* 15(1): 17–36.

Selivan, L. (2021). *Activities for alternative assessment: monitoring learning accomplishments in the ELT classroom*. Stuttgart: DELTA Publishing.

Stathopoulou, M. (2015) *Cross-language mediation in foreign language teaching and testing*, Cleveland: Multilingual Matters.

Vygotsky, L. S. (1978). *Mind in society*, Cambridge: Harvard University Press.

Wiseman, J. (2020, February 14) *Mediation* (No. 8) In Pearson English podcast. Pearson. Retrieved from: https://www.pearson.com/english/about/podcast.html.